NEW
HOTELS
FOR
GLOBAL NOMADS

NEW
HOTELS
FOR
GLOBAL NOMADS

Donald Albrecht
with Elizabeth Johnson

MERRELL

Cooper-Hewitt, National Design Museum

First published 2002 by
Merrell Publishers Limited
42 Southwark Street
London SE1 1UN

in association with

Cooper-Hewitt, National Design Museum
Smithsonian Institution
2 East 91st Street
New York, NY 10128
www.si.edu/ndm

Published on the occasion of the exhibition
New Hotels for Global Nomads
organized by Cooper-Hewitt, National Design Museum,
Smithsonian Institution, New York
October 29, 2002–March 2, 2003

Distributed in the U.S. by Rizzoli International Publications,
Inc., through St. Martin's Press, 175 Fifth Avenue, New York,
NY 10010

Produced by Merrell Publishers Limited
Designed by Alicia Yin Cheng
Edited by Elizabeth Johnson and Sarah Yates
Printed and bound in Italy

Library of Congress Cataloging-in-Publication Data:
Albrecht, Donald.
New hotels for global nomads / Donald Albrecht with Elizabeth
Johnson.
        p.   cm.
"Organized by Cooper-Hewitt, National Design Museum,
Smithsonian Institution, New York, October 29, 2002–March
2, 2003."
Includes bibliographical references and index.
ISBN 1-85894-174-1
1. Hotels—Exhibitions. 2. Hotels—Designs and plans—
Exhibitions. 3. Hotels—Decoration—Exhibitions.
4. Architecture, Modern—20th century—Exhibitions.
I. Albrecht, Donald. II. Cooper-Hewitt, National Design
Museum. III. Title.
NA7800 .A425 2002
728'.5'0747471—dc21   2002008696

02 03 04 05 / 10 9 8 7 6 5 4 3 2 1

British Library Cataloging-in-Publication Data:
Albrecht, Donald
New hotels for global nomads
1. Hotels 2. Hotels—Design 3. Architecture, Modern—
20th century
I. Title II. Cooper-Hewitt, National Design Museum
728.5'09045

ISBN 1 85894 174 1

Donald Albrecht

ACKNOWLEDGMENTS

I have long been fascinated by architecture as a cultural and social phenomenon, so the idea of curating an exhibition about hotels, which resonate with people like few other buildings, offered a golden opportunity. Seeking to capture the moment in contemporary hotel culture and present *New Hotels for Global Nomads* in the fall of 2002, only about eighteen months after I proposed the idea, required extra effort on the part of many individuals to whom I am deeply in debt. At Cooper-Hewitt, National Design Museum, Susan Yelavich, former Assistant Director for Public Programs, was the first person to support the project and she continued to serve as advisor and friend throughout much of the process. Museum Director Paul Warwick Thompson has been a great advocate as well, from the moment he assumed his new position at the Museum through the project's completion. I also appreciate the work of Jill Bloomer, who oversaw the production of new photography, which was expertly taken by Matt Flynn. Dorothy Dunn, Jennifer Brundage, Monica Hampton, and Mei Mah of the education department developed stimulating programs. Given the large number of custom installations within the exhibition, its physical presentation was daunting. Architecture Research Office (ARO), specifically Stephen Cassell, Elizabeth Huck, and Rosalyne Shieh, designed a visually spectacular and intelligent installation, which was dramatically lit by Mary Ann Hoag. ARO's Ben Fuqua designed the wonderful New York Nature Hotel. The exhibition's graphic design was creatively conceived and implemented by the Museum's design department, headed by Alicia Cheng and Jen Roos, and developed by Yve Ludwig. None of their wonderful designs could have been realized, however, were it not for the production management led by Lindsay Stamm Shapiro with Jocelyn Groom and Scott Wilhelme, who oversaw an expert construction crew, especially Mathew Weaver. Essential support for the project was also provided by Jennifer Northrop, Phoebe Bell, Lois Woodyatt, Linda Dunne, Erin Young, Steven Langehough, and Jeff

McCartney. Caroline Baumann and Kris Herndon took on the difficult job of fundraising with energy and flair. I thank our sponsors at the time of writing this, Loews Hotels, Maharam, Kimpton Boutique Hotels, Waterworks, and Marlene Meyersohn. Maharam's ongoing support of my projects is especially rewarding.

Exhibitions of contemporary work also demand the perspective of eyes beyond my own. I am especially grateful to Thomas Reynolds, Joseph Holtzman, Susan Yelavich, Caroline Baumann, and Norman Kleeblatt for bringing great projects to my attention.

New Hotels for Global Nomads is the first book Cooper-Hewitt, National Design Museum has published with Merrell. Our excellent relationship with Hugh Merrell, Julian Honer, Matt Hervey, and Anthea Snow demonstrates that there will be many more collaborations. I especially thank Alicia Cheng for the book's beautiful and lucid design, as well as for her patience in working on endless revisions.

Phyllis Ross and Randi Mates provided expert research skills and capacity to handle myriad details. Although Floramae McCarron-Cates and Todd Olson joined the team in midstream, they nonetheless were essential to its completion. Natalie Shivers, as always, was instrumental in shaping and clarifying ideas for the book and the show, as well as editing my introductory essay. I am also deeply grateful to the work Elizabeth Johnson gave the book, as coauthor, general editor, and friend with a great sense of humor. Friends and family have also been mainstays of support and counsel.

Finally, exhibitions are as much about creative people as they are about creative process. It has been an especially enriching experience discovering and collaborating with the talented architects, designers, photographers, and artists who comprise the heart of *New Hotels for Global Nomads*.

Paul Warwick Thompson

PREFACE

DIRECTOR, COOPER-HEWITT, NATIONAL DESIGN MUSEUM

Hotels are buildings that have been reinvented and reimagined for nearly two hundred years—now more so than ever. Since the nineteenth century, hotels, whether in cities or remote oases, have evolved from simple places to sleep while on the road into elaborate destinations that combine private guestrooms with restaurants, lounges, gyms, spas, meeting facilities, and ballrooms. Architecture has become experience. *New Hotels for Global Nomads* brings together an international selection of architects and designers who have created contemporary hotel culture, and artists who have interpreted it. Published just over a year after the terrorist attacks of 2001, this book and the accompanying exhibition demonstrate that travel and tourism remain central to modern life.

A vast team has made this project possible, but special thanks go to Merrell Publishers; Alicia Cheng, book and exhibition graphics designer; Elizabeth Johnson, book coauthor and editor; and Donald Albrecht, who conceived and curated the show.

Donald Albrecht

"HERE YOU MEET EVERYBODY AND EVERYBODY MEETS YOU"

As tourism and travel have become an integral part of people's social and economic lifestyles, hotels have been transformed into crossroads of our nomadic society. Geographic borders appear to have eroded as people travel anywhere anytime—for business, pleasure, or the sheer thrill of being on the move. Much of the world's population seems to be in perpetual motion, and the design of contemporary hotels has evolved to encourage this trend.

Today's hotels are not just places in which to sleep. This new generation of hotels meets tourists' increasing demands for leisure and business travelers' needs for offices on the road. They also offer escapist experiences in faraway worlds. As society expects more and more entertainment, hotels are meeting the challenge with escalating theatricality. In their artful manipulations of imagery, illusion, and perception, new venues are designed to astound and amaze with their artifice —from an "Egyptian pyramid" in Las Vegas to a high-tech "Arabian bazaar" in Dubai, and a hotel in Switzerland in which the guestroom ceilings "dissolve" into film images.

Even nature itself has been turned into a spectacle for tourists. Hotels in natural settings emerged in the nineteenth century to provide respites from city life and industrialization.

Today's "natural" hotels continue this tradition, offering places to detox from stress and routine. Eco-tourist spas feature pristine habitats and wildlife, while some sites appealing to the extreme tourist accommodate guests in hotels made entirely of ice or provide jumping-off points for high-risk sports. Tourism in even the final frontier of the natural environment—outer space—is becoming a real possibility in the twenty-first century.

Apart from their capacity to provide entertainment and relaxation, modern hotels are essential in today's global economy, functioning as depots on a vast network of digitally connected sites. These hotels have become, in effect, modular capsules outfitted with state-of-the-art technology. People conduct more business in a worldwide marketplace, and the geographic range of commerce has expanded greatly. Hotels have followed. Airplanes making long-distance flights now act as mobile hotels, offering bed-like reclining seats and a wide variety of in-flight entertainment.

New Hotels for Global Nomads brings together approximately thirty-five projects that forecast directions for the development of hotels in the twenty-first century. Taking its cue from five themes that have defined the historical evolution of hotels—urbanism, mobility, busi-

ness, nature, and fantasy—this book spotlights contemporary architects, artists, and designers who have reinterpreted and reinvented this centuries-old building type with remarkable flair.

URBAN HOTELS

The modern hotel was a product of epochal changes throughout the Western world in the early nineteenth century. The American and French revolutions signaled the decline of the aristocracy and the rise of a mercantile bourgeoisie. Coalescing and expanding as a class with its own identity, this group created new industries, and new modes of communication and transportation. The bourgeoisie also introduced a new concept—leisure time—that led to the development of the modern tourist industry.

At the same time the size of cities increased exponentially. London, Paris, New York, and soon Tokyo grew into major metropolises. New types of buildings emerged to accommodate new ways of living and doing business. Office buildings housed hundreds of workers. Shopping arcades fulfilled the bourgeoisie's desire to consume novel goods. Hotels met the population's growing mobility and provided public arenas for the grand—and not-so-grand—to see and be seen.

During this period the opening of a new hotel signified a city's economic and cultural coming-of-age. Competition for hotel business was fierce, not only *within* a particular city but *between* cities themselves.[01] Hotel owners and managers sought to outdo each other however they could. Grander architecture signaled the modern hotel's new-found stature. Hotels became destinations in themselves, not just waystations for travelers *en route*. People of all classes were attracted by their lavishly appointed public spaces (no longer the sole province of private clubs and mansions of the rich), private room amenities, and novel technology such as electric lights and early intercom systems.

Charles Dickens, an acute observer of contemporary mores, was among the first authors to extol the urban hotel as an icon of the industrial age. Boston's Tremont House, Dickens

noted in his 1842 travel journal *American Notes for General Circulation*, "has more galleries, colonnades, piazzas, and passages than I can remember, or the reader would believe."[02] It also had more rooms (170) than the traditional inn, which had housed no more than thirty only a few decades earlier.[03] Opened in 1829, the Tremont House laid the foundation for the modern urban hotel in other ways. Inns had been designed by local builders, but modern hotels like the Tremont required the efforts of professional architects who could provide a strong visual identity and coordinate complex structural, mechanical, and electrical systems. Designed by one of the nation's leading architects, Isaiah Rogers, the Tremont featured a white granite facade in neo-classical style. It filled an entire block on Tremont Street and established the aristocratic palace as the model for hotel architecture. Its public spaces, with their high ceilings and marble-mosaic floors, offered guests the illusion of living, if only temporarily, like kings and queens. Bellhops carried guests' luggage upstairs, where the halls and guestrooms were carpeted and the windows curtained. Guests enjoyed the use of washbowls and free soap in their rooms, setting the trend for complimentary toiletries. (The courtyard housed eight bathrooms, an unusually generous number for the time.) Each of the Tremont's rooms had lockable doors, offering guests greater privacy than the traditional inn, where people slept in a single communal room or separated from one another by flimsy screens.

Small innovations such as locks on hotel rooms reflected big changes in society. The sense of individuality that private rooms and locked doors provided was central to the identity of the emerging middle class who patronized hotels such as the Tremont. Industrial mass production was unleashing a flood of standardized goods and a rising discomfort with total uniformity. Consequently, personal identification, expression, and privacy gained greater importance. Locks were not the only innovation at the Tremont that facilitated privacy. At other hotels guests had to present themselves at the main desk to get assistance or meet visitors. From their private rooms at the Tremont, however, guests could use Seth Fuller's newly invented "annunciator" to communicate with the front desk. When pressed, a button in the room activated a small hammer and gong at the desk, which in turn vibrated a card printed with the room number.

The Tremont also advanced the hotel's rise as a business enterprise. By increasing the number of rooms and standardizing them into repetitive rentable units, the owners and designers of early nineteenth-century urban hotels created "consumable space"—an economic concept that underlies hotel financing even today.[04] (Japanese capsule hotels, which are composed of refrigerator-sized, stackable units, are an extreme version of this model.) Like office buildings and shopping arcades, hotels were divided into modules, the size of which represented the minimal space that could be rented at the maximum price. At the Tremont the private floors were systematically divided into rooms that each cost a flat rate of $2 a day. This price, as much as four times the going rate for other hotels, was a deliberate attempt to keep out the poorer classes.[05]

The Tremont also spurred widespread hotel envy among entrepreneurs in other cities. Not to be outdone by Boston, New York financier John Jacob Astor hired Isaiah Rogers to design the Astor House in lower Manhattan, which surpassed the Tremont in size, cost, and sumptuousness. Rogers quickly became a sought-after architect and was called upon to design hotels in numerous cities across the United States, often reusing the neo-classical model that had served him well in Boston and New York.

Hotels such as the Tremont and the Astor established the building type as a laboratory for new technologies. Manufacturers sometimes tested ideas such as central heating and electricity in hotels before introducing them to the domestic market. As "homes away from home" hotels offered inventors the chance to let the public try out their new devices without asking people to buy them. Thus hotels boast a long list of inventive initiatives. America's first public

New York's Hotel Broadway, designed by Jean Nouvel and Antonio Citterio, marries the modern boutique and the grand hotel tradition.

Architects and designers have turned hotels into fantasy environments by manipulating scale, creating dramatic lighting, and juxtaposing wildly diverse period styles. Dorothy Draper, America's high priestess of theatrical chic, applied her signature style of neo-baroque decoration and bold overlapping pattern to the interior design of the Quitandinha Hotel in Petropolis, Brazil, in 1944 (this page and opposite, top). Philippe Starck and Anda Andrei render the style contemporary in London's Sanderson Hotel (opposite, below).

building with steam-powered heating was Boston's Eastern Exchange Hotel (1846). Londoners first rode passenger elevators in the new Westminster Palace Hotel (1861). And in 1882, only three years after Thomas Edison's invention of the incandescent bulb, New York's Hotel Everett became the first electrified American hotel. The public was dazzled as 101 bulbs lit the Everett's grand public rooms.[06]

Electric lights, steam-powered heating, grand public spaces, and clean rooms were not the only means hotel entrepreneurs used to attract guests, who demanded higher levels of service from modern hotels than they did from older inns. Hoteliers developed two types of service to meet these needs. The European plan of hotel operation, which originated in France, charged guests only for their rooms. Meals were paid for separately, whether guests chose to dine in their own rooms via "room service," or in the hotel's public restaurants. Under the American plan the price of the room included meals. Before the 1870s only a few hotels in New York and other large Eastern cities offered the European plan. Special guests at the Tremont House could insist upon certain features of the European plan, such as room service and *à la carte* dining, in which food was cooked and served to order, rather than the American preference for *table d'hôte,* in which a fixed bill-of-fare was served all at once to the entire table. Throughout the mid-nineteenth century, Americans resisted the European plan as an attack on the nation's democratic ideals. To poet and journalist Nat P. Willis, communal dining in the public rooms of hotels was "the tangible republic—the only thing palpable and agreeable that we have to show, in common life, as republican."[07] Nevertheless, the American plan soon disappeared and today it is largely confined to cruise ships and certain resorts.

By drawing people out of their homes and into public spaces, where local residents mixed with travelers from around the world, hoteliers could transform social customs. In one celebrated example, at the end of the nineteenth century Richard D'Oyly Carte hired Swiss-born César Ritz to run London's Savoy Hotel as a way

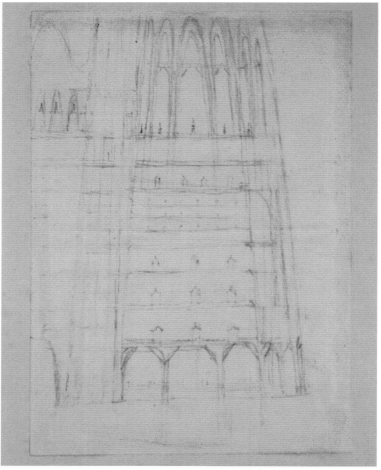

to boost business. Ritz—who had managed leading hotels in virtually every capital of Europe and would soon open the Ritz in Paris—had made his name synonymous with the modern ideal of hotel service and elegance. He brought the great French chef Georges-Auguste Escoffier to the Savoy with him. Soon the trio of D'Oyly Carte, Ritz, and Escoffier wooed London society figures, who had rarely dined outside their homes, to after-theater suppers.[08]

For these new social venues hotel architects conceived grand sequences of ceremonial public spaces—from entrance vestibule to lobby to arcade to sweeping stairway. Guests moved through these spaces, and their experience was akin to traveling from one new place to another. As a means of bringing the energy of the city indoors, architects also developed the multistory atrium lobby surrounded by restaurants, shops, and balconies. This arrangement reinforced the hotel's role as a social event in a safe and weatherproof environment. Everyone participated in the drama of the building, from those awed by the atrium's exhilarating height to those riding newly invented elevators, and to guests watching the crowds from open balconies. Even Spanish architect Antoni Gaudí conceived an atrium-centered, beehive-shaped hotel (never built) for New York in 1908. John Portman's Hyatt Regency Hotel in Atlanta, completed in 1967, breathed new life into this historic tradition and spawned countless imitators.

Hotel lobbies took on social and national characteristics—at least for commentators on the nineteenth-century American scene. While traveling in the United States in 1861, English novelist Anthony Trollope noted that American hotels were surprisingly open to the general public—as open, Trollope felt, as the street. American hotels shocked even natives. Expressing his growing disenchantment with the United States, novelist Henry James disparaged American hotels for the "democratization of elegance" because all classes were allowed to commingle there, in contrast to the more class-conscious European hotels.[09] Trollope and James saw the hotel as a metaphor for the egalitarian nature of American society. Then, as

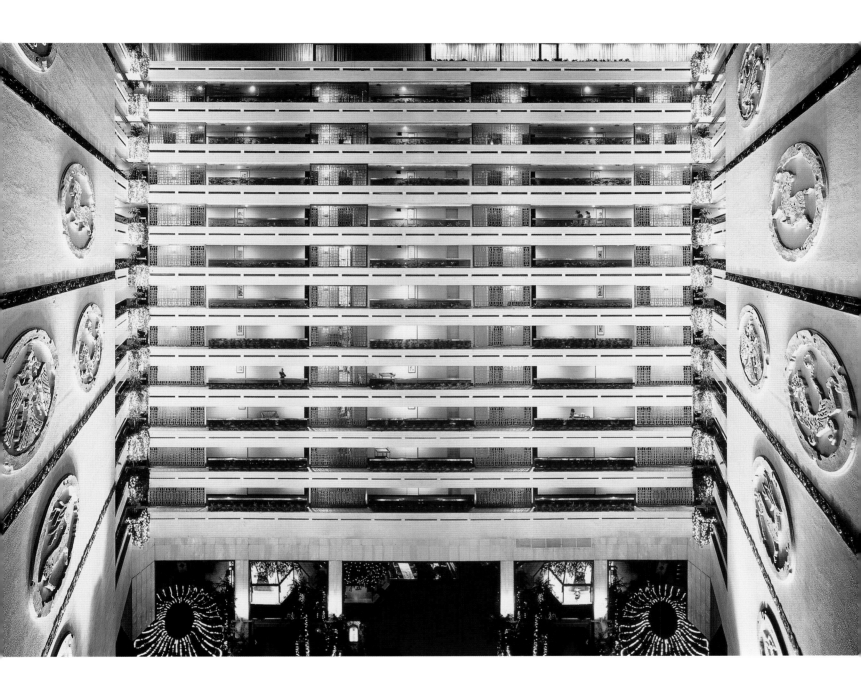

Frank Lloyd Wright's design for Tokyo's Imperial Hotel was total: the building's angular geometric forms (top) gave shape to the architect's custom-designed chairs (bottom).

today, the permeable boundaries between outside and inside, public and private, elite and common gave hotels their social thrill.

The grand hotel tradition, invented in America, quickly spread to England and France, and then around the world on the heels of colonial imperialism. As Western powers developed trading posts throughout Africa and Asia, hotels were built in such commercial centers as Bombay and Singapore to serve tourists and business travelers, symbolizing the modernity of these Asian cities. The routes of trains and ocean liners linked a network of cities with grand urban hotels. Launched in the early 1880s the Orient Express initially connected Paris and Istanbul. Then its sponsor, the French Compagnie Internationale des Wagons-Lits, built the first international chain of hotels in Nice, Monte Carlo, Lisbon, Brindisi (in Italy), and, for a brief time, Beijing. Even greater expansion became possible in 1869 when the Suez Canal opened, making travel by ocean liner easier between Europe and Asia. As a result there rose hotels that merged familiar Western architecture and conveniences with exotic "oriental" touches: Raffles in Singapore (1887) and the Taj Mahal in Bombay (1904).[10]

In the same spirit of Asian expansion and modernization, Frank Lloyd Wright's Imperial Hotel established Tokyo's status as a major city and set a new standard for avant-garde hotel design. Completed in 1922, the Imperial Hotel was a massive complex of buildings, landscaping, and pools. Wright ornamented the hotel's dynamic composition of horizontal spandrels and vertical piers with geometric reliefs carved into soft lava stone. At the hub of the complex was a multistoried, nave-like lobby with balconies overlooking the main space. Wright's concept for the design was total: he custom-designed furniture as well as dinnerware for the hotel. Technologically innovative, the building survived the devastating earthquake of 1923, owing to Wright's ingenious structural system, but, sadly, was demolished in 1967. And, while Wright's style was unique, the Imperial demonstrated that hotels could be laboratories for modern architectural ideas.

The ultimate conflation of hotels and urban development was New York's Grand Central Terminal, the Beaux-Arts centerpiece of an extraordinary complex of office buildings, apartment buildings, and hotels. The terminal was railroad engineer William Wilgus's conception of a new urban real-estate development, a way to "make the land pay" more. Prior to the construction of Grand Central, land was viewed as having value on and below the surface, including rights to mineral resources. But Wilgus realized that the space over the tracks was valuable as well and invented the concept of "commercial air rights." To pay for the enormous cost of excavating this area, Wilgus proposed selling the rights to real-estate developers, who were keen to build skyscrapers over the tracks. Throughout the 1910s and 1920s Wilgus's concept of air rights was realized. Not only were such hotels as the Commodore and Biltmore part of the new "terminal city," but another—the new Waldorf-Astoria, which opened in 1931—distilled urban living and became a kind of city within the city. The Waldorf's complex of lobbies, bars, shops, restaurants, and hotel rooms as well as office spaces and apartments within an Art Deco structure has since come to represent the apogee of urban hotel development and sophistication.

Fifty years after the Waldorf opened Bill Kimpton in San Francisco and Ian Schrager and Steve Rubell in New York refurbished rundown urban hotels with style. Kimpton converted the Hotel Bedford and, a few years later, the Vintage Court. Schrager and Rubell hired Parisian Andrée Putman to transform a dowdy Manhattan hotel into the hip Morgans. Kimpton and Schrager established the template for a generation of stylish "boutique" hotels that are both urban and urbane. Serving as design palaces, social meccas, and urban jewels, three of Schrager's newest hotels—the Clift in San Francisco, and the Sanderson and St. Martins Lane in London—are highlighted in *New Hotels for Global Nomads*. Three other striking examples of the reinvented urban hotel are seen in André Balazs's proposed Hotel Broadway in

This 1937 poster depicting a cutaway view inside New York's Waldorf-Astoria Hotel, designed by Schultze & Weaver, unmasks the diverse functions that make the hotel a veritable "city-within-the-city."

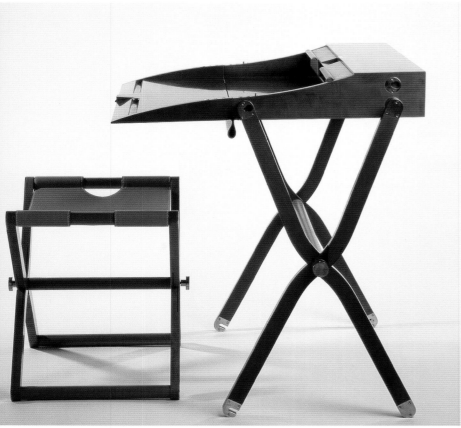

Mobility has been accommodated not only by hotels built close to transportation systems, from roads to trains to airplanes, but by mobile furniture. Hermès's 1985–87 Pippa stool and desk (top), designed by Rena Dumas and Peter Coles, converts from carrying case to hotel-room office, while Pierre Savorgnan de Brazza, explorer of the Congo, used an identical model of this 1879 Louis Vuitton bed-trunk (bottom).

New York City, and the Loews Philadelphia and Metropolitan Hotel. Richard Barnes's provocative photographs expose the machinery of Las Vegas, while conceptual projects by Servo, fieldOFFICE, and nARCHITECTS point to the next generation.

HOTELS ON THE MOVE

The oldest inns were waystations for traders along the fabled Silk Road and for pilgrims to Mecca and Rome. These ancient accommodations were spaced apart no more than the distance people or animals could walk in a day. Travel over greater distances became possible only in the nineteenth century with the coming of the railroad, the first means of mechanical locomotion. No invention transformed modern life, and hotel culture with it, like the railroad. It revolutionized our sense of time and space, connecting nations as never before into vast networks serving new business and leisure activities. Beginning around 1840, urban hotels would be constructed close to—or even physically connected to—the grand railroad terminals that symbolized modern urban life. Railroad cars themselves served as traveling hotels for tourists and businesspeople alike, who enjoyed comfortable sleeping compartments and elegant dining-cars. Railroads also offered people a fast and convenient way to escape the city. Outside the confines of urban life, people could encounter nature, which was considered a nurturing force and a necessary antidote to urban ills. The ability to take the train and discover such previously inaccessible natural wonders as mountains, forests, and lakes spurred the development of leisure time as a way of life for the new middle class, the clientele for some of the earliest chain hotels.

The first wave of railroad hotels arose primarily in Britain, where the Industrial Revolution began, and miles of track soon linked virtually every city. Because British railroads were privately owned, they competed with one another for business. Low fares, comfortable seats, and convenient hotels were all means of attracting passengers. Fine hotels soon sprang up near railroad stations around the country.[11]

As the nation's capital London was the hub of railroad hotels. The first trains arrived in 1836, followed soon after by spectacular stations such as King's Cross and Paddington. At the latter the Great Western Railway built a grand hotel in about 1860, which was soon eclipsed by the efforts of competing companies. In 1862 the highly successful Midland Railway extended its lines to the capital and decided to build an imposing terminus. Engineer W. H. Barlow created the arched iron train shed of St. Pancras Station, and architect Sir George Gilbert Scott designed the adjoining Midland Grand Hotel. Opened in 1873, the hotel was clad in extravagant Gothic garb, disparagingly described at the time as "an 'advertising medium' for bagmen's bedrooms and the costly discomforts of a railway hotel."[12] Nevertheless, the Midland Grand's jagged silhouette of pointed spires and the sheer lavishness of its detailing epitomized the image of urban hotels as secular cathedrals.

Inspired by Britain, Canada developed its own system of railway hotels—the first chain hotels dependent exclusively on rail travel. In 1885 the transcontinental Canadian Pacific Railroad system was completed, linking the vast Canadian landscape from coast to coast. The Banff Springs Hotel (1888), designed by New York architect Bruce Price in the style of France's Loire Valley châteaux, set the standard for the chain's architectural identity. Other hotels soon followed, such as the Château Frontenac (1892) in Quebec and the Place Viger (1898) in Montreal.[13]

To accommodate travelers on their journeys even further, the train car itself was turned into a kind of mobile hotel. While wealthy passengers hooked their own private cars to trains, railroads sold less affluent customers the amenities they would find at station-side hotels. "Flying bedrooms" (sleeping cars) and "flying drawing rooms" (parlor cars) fascinated the nineteenth-century public, who could see ornately styled versions in popular exhibitions even if the price of train tickets was out of reach. For these hotels on wheels, innumerable patents were issued to inventors for seats that

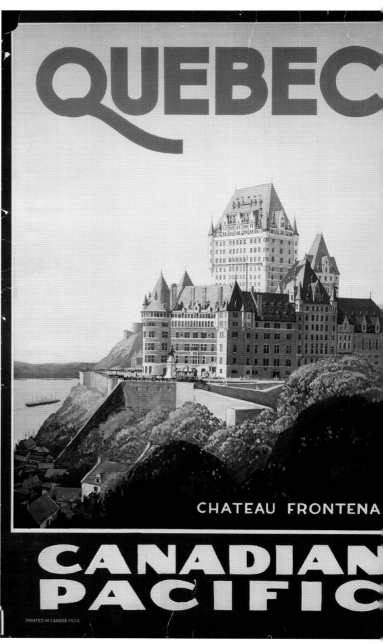

Both London's 1873 Midland Grand Hotel (left) and Quebec's 1892 Château Frontenac resulted from collaborations between railroads and hotels. Behind the neo-gothic facade of the Midland Grand Hotel lay a vast iron-and-glass railroad station, while the Frontenac was one of many hotels linked to the Canadian Pacific Railroad.

reclined or converted into beds. In 1867 George M. Pullman introduced his first hotel car on Canada's Great Western Railroad. Pullman's sleeper-car featured a small kitchen at one end, from which meals were served to the car's occupants on tables set up between their seats. Dining cars for everyone on the train soon followed. Once such amenities became commonplace, the general level of luxury on trains increased.[14] What had begun as a way to meet the simple need for a comfortable place to sleep flowered into such legendary, full-service trains as the Orient Express and the streamlined 20th Century Limited.

The concept of mobility, both metaphoric and actual, shapes the projects in this section of *New Hotels for Global Nomads*. Trucks, automobiles, and buses are the starting points, respectively, for projects conceived by Carl de Smet, Acconci Studio, and Lewis.Tsurumaki.Lewis, while space travel inspired projects by the Habitability Design Center and Hans-Jurgen Rombaut. All the projects respond to new, burgeoning, or potential facets of tourism in a mobile culture.

HOTELS AS GLOBAL BUSINESS

As early as the 1830s the public rooms of hotels had become not only places of social interaction and dining but also modern-day agoras where men conducted business. "Here you meet everybody and everybody meets you," British novelist Frederick Marryat noted when he visited America. "Here you obtain the news, all the scandal, all the politics, and all the fun."[15]

Hospitality was of great concern to the newly mobile group of salesmen, known as "commercial tourists" or "commercial travelers," who spent grueling hours in search of customers. First appearing in Britain at the end of the eighteenth century, then in America in about 1830, these men were the lifeblood of modern hotel business. They rented 75% of the rooms in commercial hotels and virtually 100% in most small-town establishments.[16] Hotel staff stayed on duty twenty-four hours a day to meet salesmen arriving hours late from delayed train connections.[17]

Some hotels were developed with the business traveler in mind. At the turn of the century American businessman Ellsworth Milton Statler launched a pioneering chain of hotels that carried his name, first in Buffalo, New York, and later in numerous cities around the country. At Statler Hotels traveling salesmen found ample facilities to meet their needs, such as ballrooms for conventions and meetings and special rooms in which they could show samples to customers. Even the lobbies could be subdivided for business purposes. Statler Hotels were among the first to have a private bathroom in each guestroom, as well as an innovative "Servidor," a shallow compartment accessible from the corridor and the room where guests placed suits and shoes to be cleaned. Hotel valets were able to pick up and return these without disturbing guests—and guests were freed from the pressure to tip. But as a convenient conduit between public hall and private room, the Servidor also could encourage mischief. The villain of Maxwell Grant's crime story "The Dead Who Lived" secretly slips a canister of poison gas into the Servidor, with near-fatal consequences for his unsuspecting victim.[18]

In building his hotels in cities throughout the country, Statler demonstrated the potential for hotels to be profitable businesses through a national network. Pioneers in the development of today's culture of restaurants and stores with outlets around the globe, chain hotels allowed entrepreneurs to maximize profits through economies of scale. Tremendous cost savings could be achieved by the parent company's purchase of furniture, linens, food, and other supplies in larger quantities than independent hotels. Economies of scale were also possible in advertising, and in reservation and cash management systems. Chains were successful because they encouraged repeat visits from customers by offering a consistent product under a trademarked name. This allowed customers to find similar accommodation all over the world, while helping hotels to achieve savings by replicating designs and operating systems.[19]

Statler Hotels started out as a national

chain served by automobiles and trains, but after World War II air travel encouraged hotel entrepreneurs to think globally. Frequent and successful flights of troops during the war made the public more secure with flying for civilian purposes in peacetime. Inexpensive "coach" fares were introduced by 1950, and jet travel about a decade later. Airplanes soon became the most popular mode of long-distance travel, leaving railroads in some countries to function primarily as transporters of freight.

Extensive air travel required new types of hotels. In 1954 Statler Hotels was bought by Hilton International (with which it eventually merged) for the astounding sum of $111 million. Among the largest real-estate transactions in history (at the time), was a sure sign that hotels were big business and that big business meant developing international chains.[20] "The function of hotels," John W. Houser, Hilton's executive vice president noted a few years later, "has now . . . been extended far beyond that [of inns and taverns] to . . . play an ever increasing role in the development of international trade and travel and in the strengthening of the economies of all countries. Hotels can offer a real contribution to economic progress by helping to bring visitors directly into contact with the products and facilities of a country."[21]

For their foreign outposts American global hotel chains created facilities that expressed both the international scope of the parent company and the local flavor of the host city. Hoteliers and architects responded with a new international style of hotel architecture, exemplified by such structures as the 1955 Istanbul Hilton. Modern materials, boxy forms, bright lighting, and interior shopping arcades identified the Hilton as a contemporary expression of American-led global culture, while public rooms designed in "exotic" local styles and using native crafts suggested Hilton was also a good and sympathetic neighbor. Conrad Hilton himself called the hotels "little Americas."[22] In his 1969 novel *Travels with My Aunt* Graham Greene suggests the safe comfort of the Hilton chain. When a distressed father learns that his teenage daughter is traveling in Kathmandu

instead of studying in London, he says, "Where's she living? I doubt if there's a good hotel in the place. If there's a Hilton at least you know where you are."[23]

These generic chains have today become so ubiquitous that they provide a cultural touchstone for designers and artists. Director Spike Jonze, architects Diller + Scofidio, and artist Dike Blair use the instantly recognizable chain hotel as a foil for witty or trenchant interpretations. In recent years, however, some hotels have begun to respond to the vast changes in business itself. Japanese capsule hotels reduce the room to its most minimal requirements and dimensions, selling little more than a compact place to sleep for Japanese workers who have missed the last train home. Joel Sanders's concept for a 24/7 Hotel Room tailors the hotel-room unit to fit the business traveler's need for a combined domestic and professional space. In acknowledgment of the frequent long-distance travel required of many businesspeople, Starwood Hotels & Resorts has developed the W chain as calming, restorative environments. Working with the Rockwell Group, it developed a brand based on the rejuvenating power of nature, so that guests may feel refreshed and invigorated after a stay in a W hotel. The Standard also furnishes a new kind of business hotel chain, for young, design-savvy travelers. They desire an edgier experience but have limited expense accounts.

NATURAL HOTELS

Introduced to the West by the ancient Greeks and perfected by the Romans, water spas were the first man-made facilities that exploited nature as a therapeutic force. Although such facilities remained popular over succeeding centuries, it was not until about 1800 that increased industrialization and urbanization made the resort valuable as a safe and hygienic component of modern life. The introduction of paid vacations would later enhance its role.

Resorts promised not only release from the stresses of modern life but fulfillment through encounters with Mother Nature. Long Branch, New Jersey, which attracted the residents of

The 1955 Istanbul Hilton, designed by Skidmore, Owings & Merrill, featured an "International Style" exterior, which expressed modern American-led global culture, while its Tulip Room lounge for women used local styles and crafts to evoke a modern-day harem.

As visual source or raw material, nature inspired such projects as Dre Wapenaar's podlike 1998 Tree Tents (top), a bench from an Adirondack mountain resort made from cedar branches (middle), and Quebec's Hôtel de Glace (Ice Hotel), where everything—from the walls to the beds—is made of ice.

both New York City and Philadelphia, was promoted in 1875 as affording "a cheap and easy release from the narrow streets of the city, and equally narrow pursuits of gain, to the soul-saving worship of the great and good God through the never-quiet, never-ceasing roar of the mighty ocean."[24]

Such resorts launched new forms of hotel architecture. With alchemists' intent, designers turned nature into tourist spectacle, and even previously unpopulated areas were converted into edens of leisure. These resorts were a totally new kind of semi-public/semi-private landscape, both wild and cultivated, that was distinct from working farms, palace gardens, and city parks. By showcasing a region's natural scenery and marketing hotels and scenery together, resort hotels helped reinforce national identity, linking America with the "Wild West," Canada with the Rockies, and Switzerland with the Alps.

Its beautiful lakes and mountains made Switzerland the first country to develop a tourist industry based on nature and sports. From the completion in 1834 of the country's first truly deluxe hotel, Geneva's Hôtel des Bergues, through World War I, waves of society's upper crust traveled on an ever-expanding network of railroads in search of romantic scenery and luxurious accommodations. After their arduous train ride, discerning travelers demanded clean rooms, attentive service, and excellent food. Swiss hoteliers excelled in providing these amenities, no one more so than César Ritz. In 1864 hotelier Johannes Caspar Badrutt launched the concept of the winter sports season when he convinced a group of British tourists that the high altitude of St. Moritz offered warm, sunny weather in winter as well as summer. Anticipating today's interest in off-the-beaten-path locations, intrepid tourists sought increasingly remote spots, and hotels sprang up to serve them. "Fashion," actress Fanny Kemble wrote in the 1870s, "directs the movements of the great majority of the people and for the last few years there has been a perfect insane rush of the whole tourist world to the valley of the Upper Engardine, to the almost

The Matterhorn overwhelms the Hotel Riffelalp, built between 1860 and 1900, with a spectacular landscape. This juxtaposition helped Switzerland launch the first tourist industry based on nature and sports.

Built to take advantage of hot springs that bubble out of nearby mountains (and that have been enjoyed by tourists since the nineteenth century), architect Peter Zumthor's Thermal Bath (1996) in Vals extends Switzerland's spa tradition into the twenty-first century. Zumthor conceived the new bath as a building that "in its entirety should seem like a great porous stone." The minimalist structure is finished in thinly cut sections of local stone.

utter forsaking of the formerly popular parts of Switzerland."[25]

The design of these hotels enhanced the experience of being in nature. Porches framed spectacular views, converting nature into a commodity to be enjoyed from a distance. Like balconies, porches also served as intermediary spaces, open to the great outdoors but still part of the hotel and, thus, civilization. Gazebos and pavilions provided outdoor spaces for dancing and other entertainments. Promenades and boardwalks at resort hotels allowed visitors to stroll along nearby waterways.

While Switzerland's "natural" hotels were often designed in a neo-classical style that emulated aristocratic mansions, nature hotels in other countries sought to blend with their settings, either physically or historically. The style of the Canadian Pacific Railroad hotels designed by Bruce Price mirrored the rugged massing of the Rocky Mountains. In America Henry Flagler launched the concept of Florida as a Spanish Colonial paradise with a series of resort hotels in a style suggesting a mythical Iberian past. Flagler's network of railroads united the eastern coast of the state from St. Augustine in the north to Palm Beach in the south.

One of the great resorts that opened the American Southwest to luxury tourism was Phoenix's Arizona Biltmore. Conceived, developed, and promoted by brothers Warren and Charles McArthur over a period of almost twelve years, the resort cost more than $2,000,000 and became the city's unrivaled jewel in the desert. Designed by the McArthurs' brother Albert Chase in a Mayan-inspired style, the hotel was constructed with an innovative system of textured, concrete blocks invented by Frank Lloyd Wright. Guests could stay in private villas, sun themselves on terraces, and dine in great restaurants. According to the *Arizona Republican* newspaper on the day the hotel opened in 1929, it was a place where people could "find solace in the desert, yet live in luxury unsurpassed."[26]

Unlike such swank resorts as the Arizona Biltmore, other hotels in the American West embodied the nation's paradoxical relationship with nature, conflating awe of the country's natural wonders with awe of humankind's capacity to tame nature. The Old Faithful Inn in Yellowstone National Park, for example, was designed in styles that imitated nature in both materials and grand scale, a relationship emphasized in advertisements that depicted hotels and mountains in similar fashion. Some hotels were even designed like rustic cabins, with beams and columns made of tree trunks and furniture constructed of branches.

New resorts continue to be developed along the same lines as their predecessors. Some hotels and facilities are specific to the local natural and built environment. Maho Bay, created by Stanley Selengut and opened on the Caribbean island of St. John in 1975, was the first eco-resort and has become a model of eco-tourism. Starting with just eighteen guest tents, it soon adopted recycled materials, used low-impact construction technology, was land-scaped with indigenous plants and powered with solar energy.

When the United Nations designated 2002 as the "International Year of Eco-Tourism" it recognized that nature-based travel is the fastest-growing segment of the tourism industry. Increasing by 20 to 30% per year, eco-tourism is an antidote to the unintended conse-quences of travel itself: mass tourism to the world's most beautiful sites can destroy what it seeks to celebrate. According to *The New York Times* in 2001, "In survey after survey, travelers say they are looking for authenticity, unfettered nature, or a chance to swim with sea mammals . . . with a clear conscience."[27]

Architecture firms such as ROY, FTL, and Architecture Research Office are ready to meet the demands of the burgeoning eco-tourism market. Their conceptual projects, included in *New Hotels for Global Nomads*, offer venues in extreme or unexpected settings—from an African river delta to New York's Central Park. Less adventurous tourists can camp in style in Dre Wapenaar's bright tents and, at Rockwell Group's Art'otel in London, enjoy nature as decor.

Promotional images of the Old Faithful Inn often emphasize the hotel's proximity to its namesake geyser, suggesting an American style of building that confronts nature on its own grand terms. The hotel was designed by Robert Reamer.

©28478—OLD FAITHFUL INN AND GEYSER, YELLOWSTONE NATIONAL PARK

COPYRIGHT BY HAYNES INC., YELLOWSTONE PARK, WYOMING

Richard D'Oyly Carte, the London impresario of Gilbert and Sullivan's operettas, brought theatrical flair to his new Savoy Hotel in 1889 by illuminating it with electric light. (Eight years earlier, D'Oyly Carte had electrified his theater with equal fanfare.) This photo from the mid-1990s illustrates the hotel has kept the tradition of dramatic lighting alive.

ALBRECHT

FANTASY HOTELS

Hotels house communities of strangers who gather outside their normal environments for brief periods. The allure of romance and sex energizes the fantasy of hotel life. The popularity of holding proms, weddings, and lovers' getaway weekends in a hotel indicates its power as a place to escape the everyday and enjoy an intensified experience. Hotels encourage people to fantasize, and, in the hands of designers from Dorothy Draper to Philippe Starck, they achieve an otherworldly, Alice-in-Wonderland quality via theatrical architecture and design. Grand stairways, glass elevators, and mysteriously lit corridors dramatize and prolong the trip to the private room, the door of which serves as the boundary between the public and private space.

Even the smallest details—such as theming the hotel staff's uniforms—have not escaped the successful hotelier's notice. Liveried door attendants, desk clerks, and elevator operators reinforced the baronial identity of grand hotels in the early nineteenth century. Brass buttons and gold braid enhanced the illusion of aristocratic taste for the new middle class patronizing modern hotels. Londoners and Parisians were the first to put staff in livery, while "democratic" America resisted until 1877, when James Breslin adopted the fashion for New York's Gilsey House. Today's uniforms are more varied, ranging from the charcoal-colored minimal styles of the sophisticated modern hotel to the themed costumes favored by Las Vegas venues.

Throughout the history of hotels, technological innovations have also helped to create a sense of fantasy. When London's Savoy Hotel opened in 1889, it was promoted as having "electric light only everywhere, ready for use at all hours of day and night." This new luxury was used throughout the hotel in the form of freestanding torchères, indirectly lit coves, and pendant fixtures. Electric light was the choice of the hotel's owner, Richard D'Oyly Carte, the impresario producer of Gilbert and Sullivan's operettas, who had created the world's first electrically lighted theater—also named the Savoy—eight years earlier, with equally newsworthy results. At the hotel, he turned guests

LEFT

Art Deco was a favorite style of urban hotels in the 1920s and 1930s, which indirectly spawned this 1930 Savoy Hotel cocktail book by Harry Craddock with designs by Gilbert Rumbold.

BELOW

The lobby of Morris Lapidus's Americana Hotel in Bal Harbor, Florida (built in 1956 by brothers Preston Robert and Laurence Tisch), featured a 40-ft-high, open-air terrarium, stocked with baby alligators and surrounded by a curvilinear wall of Aztec-style screens and massive sofas.

These souvenirs miniaturize the latest generation of Las Vegas's architecturally fantastic hotels in forms that evoke the style of each hotel's decor.

into dramatis personae before the footlights, even naming the hotel's private dining rooms after Gilbert and Sullivan's operettas.[28]

Fifty-some years after D'Oyly Carte literally brought theatrical fantasy into the hotel, Morris Lapidus was inspired by the cinema for the creation of Miami Beach and Bal Harbor hotels such as the Fontainebleau, Eden Roc, and Americana in the 1950s. "People are looking for illusions," Lapidus said of his middle-class clientele. "They don't want the world's realities. And I asked myself, where do I find this world of illusion? . . . Only one place—the movies. . . . The hell with everything else."[29] Lapidus's lobbies were grandiose, with sweeping staircases and even room-sized terrariums. His restaurants made guests feel like movie stars. At the Fontainebleau, for example, the entrance is elevated to create a dais where patrons briefly pause before descending steps into the dining room.

While Lapidus was developing his fabled Miami Beach hotels, Las Vegas rose like a mirage in the desert. The Strip, a four-mile stretch of casinos and hotels outside downtown, was inaugurated in 1941 by Thomas E. Hull's Southwestern-style El Rancho Vegas resort. Over the next twenty-five years, Las Vegas took shape as a kind of Hollywood backlot in the Western-style Frontier and the science fiction–inspired Stardust. Bugsy Siegel's Flamingo was designed by former MGM set designer Douglas Honnold in movie-musical style, and in 1966, Caesars Palace, the Roman epic of Las Vegas casino hotels, fused Cecil B. DeMille with Gian Lorenzo Bernini.

While hotels have sparked the originality of architects and hoteliers from D'Oyly Carte to Lapidus and Siegel, they have also fired the imagination of artists and writers. Charles Dickens's wonder at the Tremont has been followed by more than a century and a half of fictional hotels depicted in paintings, novels, films, and plays. In the realms of art and fiction, asymmetrical relationships between the strangers who collide within the hotel's democratic setting often spark narrative conflict. Rem Koolhaas has noted that in their public

Heart-shaped tubs, bubble baths, mirrors, and champagne are de rigeur in this 1980s advertisement for the Monarch Towers at the Mount Airy Lodge in Mt. Pocono, Pennsylvania. The ad guarantees "cool elegance" and "vibrant romance" for "those couples like you who want everything, and then some. . . ."

Hotel Suite II by *Helmut Newton, from his 1979 series Helmut Newton Sleepless Nights*

lobbies, a broad spectrum of society has moved. Random meetings between characters of different social and economic backgrounds are the basis of innumerable plots. Shopgirls and secretaries pursue or are pursued by lecherous tycoons; heiresses fall in love with poor bellhops against the protestations of their dowager mothers; or young girls squander their meager savings to spend the weekend at an expensive hotel, where they masquerade as socialites in order to hook wealthy husbands. In Thomas Mann's novella *Death in Venice* the elderly and aristocratic Gustav von Aschenbach meets and becomes obsessed by the young and beautiful Tadzio in a Venetian hotel, and Mrs. Robinson entraps Benjamin Braddock in a hotel in Mike Nichols's film *The Graduate*. Vicki Baum's 1929 novel *Grand Hotel*, later translated for the stage and screen, presents a veritable social wheel of fortune, concluding, "The revolving door turns and turns—and swings . . . and swings . . . and swings."[30]

Fictional hotels also represent a fluid sense of personal identity. In *Remembrance of Things Past*, Marcel Proust sets his hero's quest for upper-class identity in a lavish French hotel. There, selecting one's seat at the dining table— and its propinquity to wealth—can bestow a new station in life. And in a culture as rootless and mobile as that of the United States, where redefining one's identity is valued, hotels have taken on a national role. Authors as diverse as Henry James and Joan Didion have seen the hotel as providing clues to the American psyche. James believed that hotels constituted "a synonym for civilization, for the capture of conceived manners themselves," leading one "to ask if the hotel-spirit may not just be the American spirit most seeking and finding itself."[31] In Edward Hopper's paintings, hotels represent loneliness, transience, and the discon-nection between people. They sit alone in their rooms, blankly staring off into an interior world. Even when they gather as groups in the hotel lobby, they don't make eye contact.

Hotels provided the setting for many films directed by Alfred Hitchcock, who often explored the impermanence of human identity

Marcello Mastroianni in his hotel room, NYC, 1963, by Diane Arbus

and the predicament of people in transition. The obsessed police officer (Jimmy Stewart) in *Vertigo* seems to achieve the final transformation of Madeleine (Kim Novak) from slut to sophisticate in a San Francisco hotel room, while New York's Plaza Hotel is the location for the case of mistaken identity that sparks the plot of *North by Northwest*. Released the following year (1960), *Psycho* opens with a camera shot descending from high above Phoenix, approaching a hotel window, and passing through it to focus on a pair of lovers after sex. The scene conveys the thrill that a hotel offers in its capacity to transgress boundaries between the public and private realms. And of course the film's famous shower scene took place in a motel where a young woman seeks to start a new life.

Eroticism and escapism continue to charge the fantasy hotels of architects and artists today. In *New Hotels for Global Nomads* W. S. Atkins's Burj al-Arab in Dubai is a high-tech dream where Teflon meets gold leaf, while Jean Nouvel's Hotel in Lucerne, Switzerland, casts visitors as film extras. M. K. Kähne elevates the mobile bathroom into a highly polished "jewel" in a portable trunk, while Tom Sachs takes the opposite direction in his deliberately crude and minimal *Compact Full Feature Hotel Room*.

The Japanese preoccupation with privacy is explored in Peter Marlow's photo essay about the country's "love hotels," which offer their visitors a thrilling game of hide-and-seek. Toland Grinnell fantasizes about the secret life of the affluent traveler in his *Private Dancer*, and Sophie Calle actually pries into the lives of hotel guests in her work of art, *The Hotel*. These artists interpret the urge to penetrate the hotel's boundary between private and public. They underscore an essential feature of the hotel experience that architects, artists, and designers understand. Ever since the Tremont House offered its guests locks and keys, the desire to know what is happening behind closed doors has increased. Although the doors are all the same, no two stories are alike.

The opening credits of Alfred Hitchcock's 1960 film Psycho *dissolve into this scene, depicting the hotel as a place of transgressive boundaries and illicit behavior. In the final frame depicted here, Janet Leigh's character looks up at her lover, played by John Gavin.*

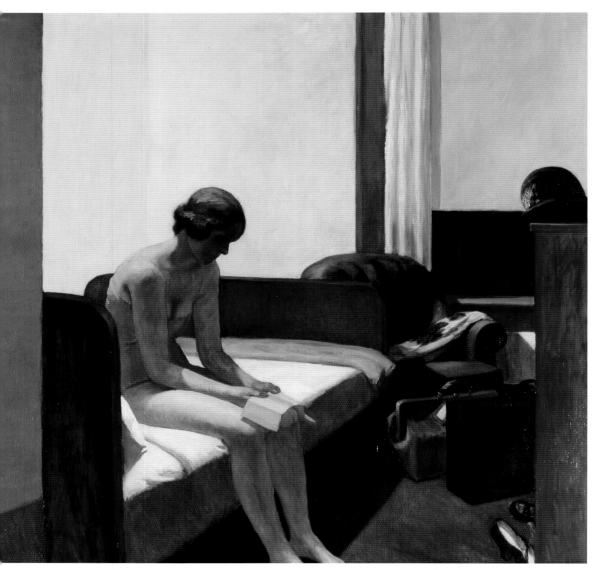

Hotel Room (1931), by Edward Hopper. Befitting her hotel-room setting, the subject of Hopper's painting is caught in a reflective moment of transition, but the particulars are left ambiguous. It is unclear whether she is undressing for bed or dressing to leave, and whether the packed suitcases belong to her or a departing lover.

ALBRECHT

NOTES

01 Karl B. Raitz and John Paul Jones III, "The City Hotel as Landscape Artifact and Community Symbol," *Journal of Cultural Geography*, IX, no. 1, 1988, pp. 17–36.

02 Charles Dickens, *American Notes for General Circulation* [1842], London and New York (Penguin Classics) 2000, p. 3.

03 Jefferson Williamson, *The American Hotel: An Anecdotal History* [1930], New York (Arno Press) 1975, p. 3.

04 Dell Upton, *The Architecture of the United States*, New York (Oxford University Press) 1988, p. 233.

05 *New York Weekly Mirror*, Dec. 7, 1844, quoted in Williamson, *American Hotel*, note 3, p. 28.

06 Many books, including Williamson, *American Hotel*, provide these kinds of statistics.

07 Ibid., pp. 208–10.

08 Elaine Denby, *Grand Hotels: Reality and Illusion*, London (Reaktion Books) 1998, pp. 144–45.

09 Noted by James in the early 1870s and quoted in Carol Berens, *Hotel Bars and Lobbies*, New York (McGraw-Hill) 1997, p. 28.

10 Joseph Fitchett, Anthony Lawrence, and Martin Meade, *Grand Oriental Hotels*, New York (Vendome Press) 1987, pp. 13–19.

11 Denby, *Grand Hotels*, note 8, pp. 45–46.

12 Quoted in Sir John Summerson, *The Architecture of Victorian England*, Charlottesville (University Press of Virginia) 1976, pp. 48–52.

13 Denby, *Grand Hotels*, pp. 165–71.

14 Early railroad history is the subject of such books as August Mencken, *The Railroad Passenger Car: An Illustrated History of the First Hundred Years with Accounts by Contemporary Passengers*, Baltimore (Johns Hopkins University Press) 1957; Stanley Buder, *Pullman: An Experiment in Industrial Order and Community Planning*, New York (Oxford University Press) 1967; and John F. Stover, *The Routledge Historical Atlas of the American Railroad*, New York and London (Routledge) 1999.

15 Carolyn E. Brucken, "Consuming Luxury: Hotels and the Rise of Middle-Class Public Space, 1825–1860," Ph.D. diss., George Washington University, 1997, p. 209.

16 Williamson, *American Hotel*, p. 124.

17 Margaret Kent Onion, "Drummers Accommodated: A Nineteenth Century Salesman in Minnesota," *Minnesota History* XLVI, no. 2, 1978, pp. 59–65.

18 Maxwell Grant, "The Dead Who Lived," *Shadow Magazine*, Oct. 1, 1938.

19 Paul Ingram, *The Rise of Hotel Chains in the United States, 1896–1980*, New York and London (Garland Publishing) 1996, p. 29.

20 From *History of the Lodging Industry*, website of the American Hotel and Lodging Association, Information Center (http://www.ahma.com/infocenter/lodging_history.asp).

21 Alexander Koch, *Hotelbauten, Motels, Ferienhäuser*, Stuttgart (Koch) 1958, p. 9.

22 This analysis of Hilton Hotels is indebted to Annabel Jane Wharton, *Building the Cold War: Hilton International Hotels and Modern Architecture*, Chicago (University of Chicago Press) 2001.

23 Graham Greene, *Travels with My Aunt*, New York (Penguin Books) 1969, p. 194.

24 Williamson, *American Hotel*, p. 249.

25 Quoted in Denby, *Grand Hotels*, pp. 111–12.

26 *Arizona Republican*, Feb. 23, 1929.

27 Timothy Egan, "Uneasy Being Green: Tourism Runs Wild," *New York Times*, May 20, 2001, Travel section, pp. 10, 12.

28 Graham Vickers, *Savoy Lights: Pentagram Papers 29*, London and New York (Pentagram Design) n.d. (c. 2000), n.p.

29 Morris Lapidus, "Now, Once and For All, Know Why I Did It," *Progressive Architecture*, Sept. 1970, p. 120.

30 Vicki Baum, *Grand Hotel* [originally published as *Menschen im Hotel*, Berlin, 1929], transl. Basil Creighton, Garden City, New York (Doubleday, Doran and Co.), 1931, p. 309.

31 Henry James, *The American Scene*, London (Chapman and Hall) 1907, p. 102.

Film stills, depicting scenes of tension and sex, are rendered on the guestroom ceilings at The Hotel in Lucerne, Switzerland.

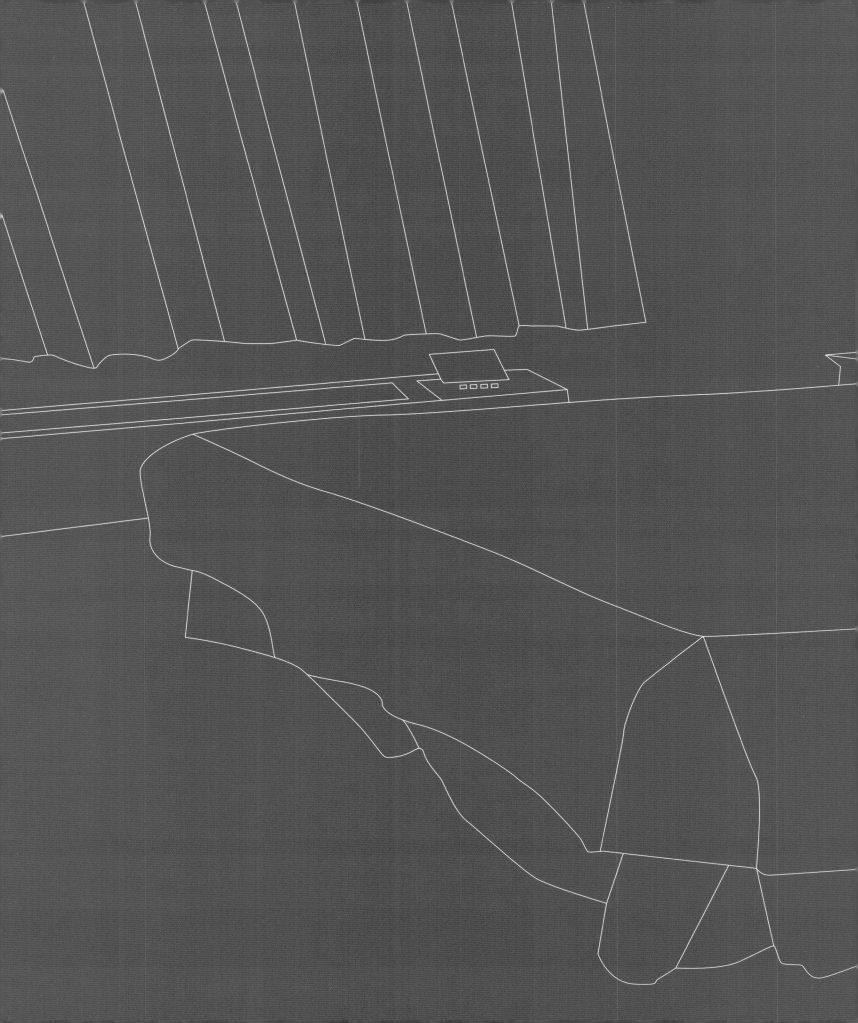

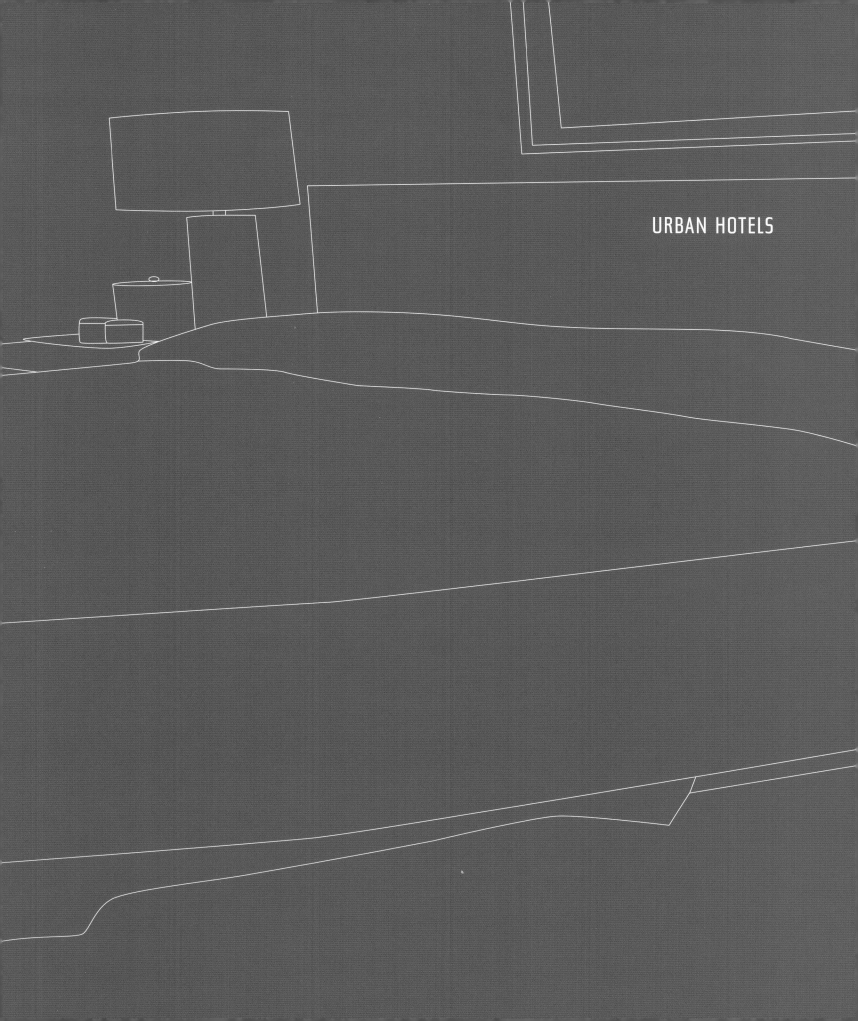

URBAN HOTELS

Philippe Starck and Anda Andrei

CLIFT SAN FRANCISCO 2001
SANDERSON LONDON 2000
LONDON 2000 # ST. MARTINS LANE

Ian Schrager is the *eminence grise* of, and the man most publicly associated with, the urban "boutique" hotel. Small, unique, and ultra-fashionable, boutiques launched the current resurgence of hotels as design palaces, social meccas, and urban jewels. For Schrager's clientele the Royalton *is* New York, the Delano is Miami, and the Mondrian is Los Angeles. Schrager recently took his highly successful brand of hotel—now numbering nine—to San Francisco with the Clift, and to London with the Sanderson and St. Martins Lane.

Schrager and then–business partner Steve Rubell began by opening Morgans in New York City in 1984. With interiors by French designer Andrée Putman, Morgans was intimate and casually elegant in the style of a British gentlemen's club, with black-and-white marble floors, leather club chairs, and wood-paneled walls. Then, with New York's Paramount in 1988, Schrager went theatrical, hiring Philippe Starck. He and Anda Andrei, Schrager's President of Design, have been responsible for the design of Schrager's hotels ever since. Reviving the tradition of the hotel as a fantasy venue, Schrager's inns have become tourist destinations in their own right, as well as gathering spots for stylish local residents. The lobbies, bars, lounges, and restaurants are designed for maximum visual intensity, with overscaled baroque furniture (juxtaposed with modern styles and materials); backlit, luminous walls and floors; and lots of billowing draperies.

This focus on the hotel's social dimension can be tracked to both Schrager's and Starck's backgrounds in nightclubs. Schrager was co-founder, with Rubell, of New York's legendary 1970s discotheque Studio 54, and Starck got his start designing the Parisian nightclub Les Bains Douches in the mid-1980s. In effect, Schrager's hotels are Studio 54 with guestrooms in the back. These rooms, beautifully designed but deliberately small, encourage guests to spend more time in the hotel's public spaces, which he has totally reinvented. "I consider myself more in the entertainment business than the hotel business," Schrager has said. "I don't sell sleep. I sell magic."
—*Elizabeth Johnson*

LEFT

The floor-to-ceiling windows in the St. Martins Lane guest-rooms offer panoramic views of the surrounding Covent Garden section of London.

BELOW

At San Francisco's historic Clift hotel, Philippe Starck and Anda Andrei's lobby features an enormous chair, custom-designed by Starck in gilt and bronze and upholstered in an antique tapestry.

The architecturally daring steel-and-colored-glass facade of the Hotel Broadway in New York evokes the groundbreaking nineteenth-century cast-iron buildings that surround it.

Ateliers Jean Nouvel and Antonio Citterio & Partners

HOTEL BROADWAY

A new hotel in the historic Manhattan neighborhood of Soho marries the boutique and grand hotel traditions. The hotel is the brainchild of hotelier André Balazs, owner of the nearby seventy-five-room Mercer, the sixty-three-room Chateau Marmont in Los Angeles, and the Standard hotels. It will be tailored to the fashion-conscious market of the boutique hotel but have more rooms (180) and more services (meeting rooms, restaurants, and a spa). And unlike boutiques, which traditionally reuse existing historic buildings, the Hotel Broadway will be built from the ground up as an innovative architectural statement in its own right.

To achieve his vision Balazs commissioned Parisian Jean Nouvel as architect and Milanese Antonio Citterio as interior architect. Nouvel's challenge was to balance two opposing forces: the building's full-block frontage demanded a bold main facade, but the site's location in one of New York's oldest and most fiercely protected historic districts required a contextual response. The solution consists of large, deeply recessed window bays that echo those of the surrounding buildings but are fabricated in ultra-modern steel and colored glass, free of historical ornament. Nouvel's design projects the romance of progressive architecture, capturing the revolutionary spirit of Soho's nineteenth-century cast-iron buildings.

The hotel's massing responds to the neighborhod's low-rise structures, which don't block out sunlight. Nouvel's floor-to-ceiling windows let abundant natural light into the rooms. Privacy is achieved by using glass "fritted" with dense patterns of dots, which are tinted different colors for different facades: blue facing Broadway, and red on the opposite elevation, reflecting nearby brick walls.

Behind the large windows the rooms are unusually spacious. Citterio's furniture is minimal and streamlined, keeping the guests' attentions on the framed views of the city outside. Many travelers, whether for business or leisure, seek a pampering experience. Because much of a guest's waking time in his or her room is spent in the bathroom, Citterio has emphasized it as a place of luxurious and sensuous retreat. Bathrooms are integrated into the rooms rather than treated as walled-off spaces, a reference to the area's tradition of residential lofts. In some cases massive, sculptural, freestanding tubs sit in the room itself.

Both Nouvel and Citterio are master manipulators of the dual properties of reflection and transparency of glass. On the ground floor the windows reflect the spectacle of the street. Within the rooms the fritted glass varies from semi-opaque to transparent: now you see into the neighbors' windows, now you don't. In their Hotel Broadway the architects create a building that is a seductive veil and intensify the urban hotel's voyeuristic allure.

—E.J.

LEFT

In the hotel's guestrooms, interior architect Antonio Citterio has placed a sculptural tub in the sleeping area, elevating the roles of bathing and exhibitionism in the modern hotel experience.

RIGHT

Two views of the Hotel Broadway underscore its smooth fit within its historic context while remaining completely modern in architectural expression. The hotel's window glass is "fritted" with dots of different colors, signifying different street facades. The section drawing shows that the height of the building's base aligns with neighboring structures.

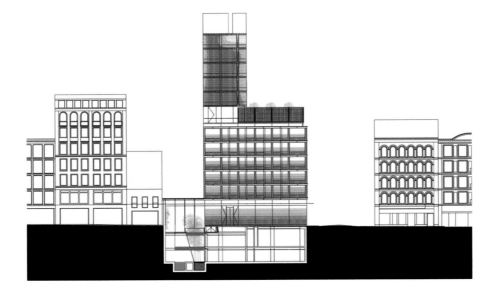

Bower Lewis Thrower Architects and Daroff Design

LOEWS PHILADELPHIA HOTEL
THE METROPOLITAN HOTEL

Loews Hotels

The cachet of mid-twentieth-century modernist architecture is a recognized asset among today's leading hoteliers, and one of the jewels in America's crown of skyscrapers is the PSFS (Philadelphia Saving Fund Society) Building in Philadelphia. When it opened in 1932, *Architectural Forum* magazine rhapsodized, "If architecture is frozen music, the Society has gone Gershwin." Recognized immediately as a masterpiece of modern design, PSFS would, within a few years, be considered the progenitor of the post-war American steel-and-glass skyscraper. Designed by William Lescaze and George Howe, PSFS is once again at the forefront of a trend: the conversion of historic office buildings into fashionable urban hotels. The transformation is achieved seamlessly because these buildings are centrally located, their floor plans are ideal for dividing into hotel rooms, they have beautiful architectural details, and their grand corporate spaces—boardrooms and executive suites—translate easily into a hotel's meeting rooms and reception halls. PSFS's most prominent feature—a dark-green granite main banking floor with huge windows wrapping its rounded corners—now serves as the hotel's most spectacular ballroom.

In their renovations Bauer Lewis Thrower Architects and Daroff Design carefully preserved and restored many of PSFS's finest details,

adhering to the intent of Jonathan M. Tisch, chairman and CEO of Loews Hotels, to respect the building's great history while breathing new life into it. The original architects created a cohesive whole by lavishing design attention on every element, including desktop accessories, light fixtures, and even clocks by Cartier, throughout the building. Loews Hotels's regard for the building's original details extends to the 8 m (27 ft) tall sign on top. But Loews went beyond simply preserving the visible and familiar PSFS sign atop the building and incorporated the PSFS logo into the hotel's own logo. The jazzy design aesthetic of the building's era inspired new furnishings such as carpets and the bar, lending a high-spirited air to the otherwise somber former bank.

A later, more flamboyant era of modernism was the inspiration for Loews' renovation of New York's Summit Hotel, originally designed in 1961 for Jonathan Tisch's father and uncle by Morris Lapidus. Having worked with the legendary Lapidus on their Americana Hotel near Miami Beach, the Tisches wanted to bring Lapidus's flair to Manhattan. Today the Summit has been renamed the Metropolitan Hotel. The building's eight-story sign and blue-green serpentine exterior are being restored, reinfusing the building with a spirit of 1960s mod.
— *Donald Albrecht*

The double-height, granite-clad banking hall of the former PSFS bank provides a monumental corner for the new Loews Philadelphia Hotel. The Loews signage employs a typeface designed for the original 1932 building.

LEFT

The former bank's furnishings, from an imposing safe to a custom-designed Cartier clock in the ground-floor elevator lobby, add modernist luster to the new hotel.

BELOW

Millennium Hall, one of the hotel's ballrooms, formerly served as the PSFS banking hall. Tall columns are clad in polished black granite. Coves of indirect lighting, used throughout the building, were fashionable expressions of modernity when the building opened in 1932.

Newly designed carpeting brings bright color and bold geometric pattern, inspired by the building's original era, to the hotel's reception lobby.

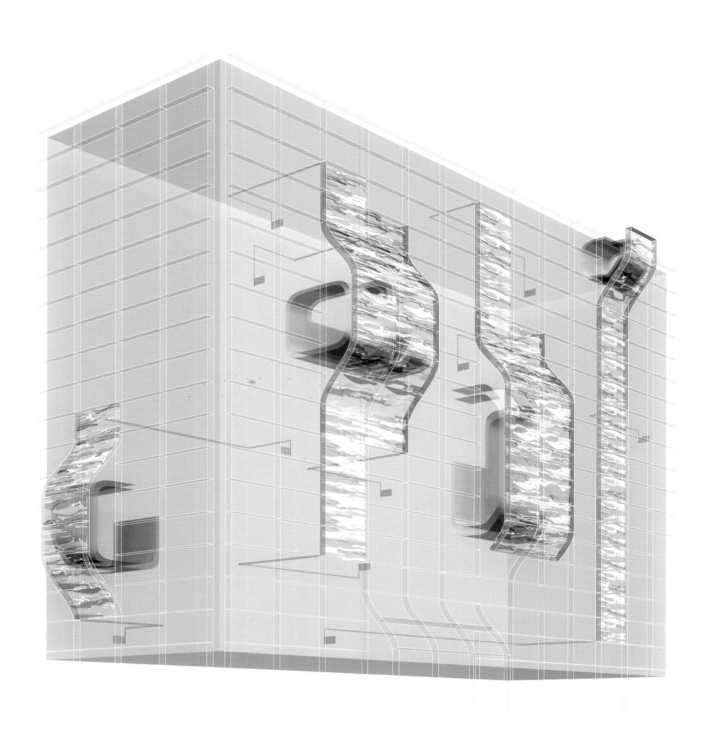

Servo

LOBBI_PORTS

2000

Conceived by the collaborative architectural practice Servo and presented for the first time in *New Hotels for Global Nomads*, Lobbi_Ports update the hotel lobby as civic space and media interface. It is a system of capsules or pods that hotel developers and architects can attach to the structure of existing hotels to provide additional high-rise lounges and observation decks. Each Lobbi_Port unit comprises a curvaceous exterior envelope or "cloudcurtain" and an interior liner and furniture system that the designers have drawn from their "nurbline" product catalog.

Servo initially developed the semitransparent cloudcurtain as a modern replacement for metal-and-glass curtain-walls, such as those on mid-twentieth-century skyscrapers, that have become both physically and environmentally obsolete. More than just a wall, cloudcurtain is a "smart skin." It can carry conduits for information technologies—improving the

building's communications capabilities—as well as electronic messages and advertising imagery that convert it into a rentable billboard. Servo's nurbline systems operate in three ways: as architecture, display system, and furniture. The interlocking display system moves on rails or wheels and can function as hotel bar or shop counter. The furniture system, designed to be digitally fabricated out of wood or acrylic in a wide range of colors and fabrics, accommodates sitting, lounging, and sleeping.

Servo has expanded on the hotel lobby's renewed appeal as a destination for both city residents and hotel guests, as seen in boutique hotels. But unlike other hotel lobbies, which are fixed parts of the ground floor, Lobbi_Ports are architectural accessories. Built from a kit of physical and digital products, Lobbi_Ports multiply and disperse this essential hotel space and the social interactions it fosters. —*D.A.*

The proposed Lobbi_Ports, a system of curvilinear capsules, offer hoteliers and architects the opportunity to attach new sky lounges and lobbies to existing structures, adding places for socializing throughout the hotel.

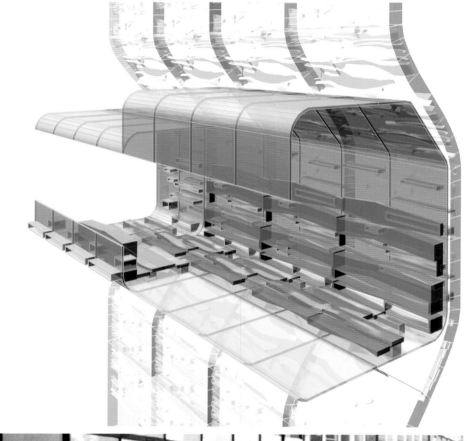

Lobbi_Ports (middle) are a kit-of-parts comprising a curvaceous exterior envelope, or "cloudcurtain," and a furniture system that can function as a seat or bed (top) or as a wall of display shelves (bottom).

Cloudcurtain is a "smart skin," carrying conduits for information technologies serving computer terminals within the hotel as well as for electronic messages and advertising on the exterior.

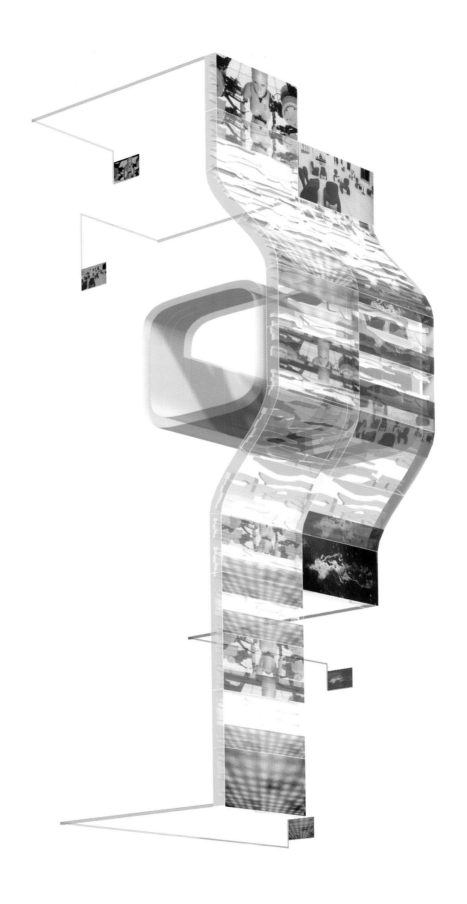

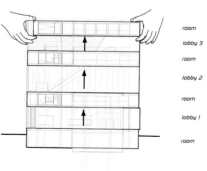

room
lobby 3
room
lobby 2
room
lobby 1
room

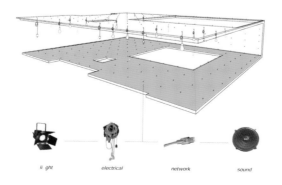

li ght   electrical   network   sound

w/c   bed   dressing   storage

URBAN HOTELS

fieldOFFICE and nARCHITECTS

HOTEL PRO FORMA

ØRESTAD CITY, DENMARK 1999

When the Danish performance group Hotel Pro Forma decided to commission a building of their own in Ørestad City, outside Copenhagen, they wanted the architecture to reflect the aesthetic of interference in their work. "Because space, concept, collaborators, and performers vary from one production to the next," says the group, each performance is unique. As a "nomadic" theater group, Hotel Pro Forma is "in constant motion."

A competition for the building was held, the first phase of which was won by a team of two New York–based firms: fieldOFFICE, headed by Annette Dudek and Jamie Meunier, and nARCHITECTS, under the direction of Eric Bunge and Mimi Hoang. Their design, also called Hotel Pro Forma, intertwines hotel, theater, and exhibition spaces. It also encourages chance encounters between different users: the Hotel Pro Forma troupe itself; visiting theater artists, who rent space for practice and performance; and typical guests attending these performances. Virtual guests participate via webcasts.

Because the amount of space given over to each of these functions varies from day to day, the hotel responds accordingly in both its public and its private spaces. The architects see the lobby of a standard hotel as "the primary locus of both scripted and spontaneous 'performances' between guests and staff." To increase the frequency of these interactions, they have devoted three of the Hotel Pro Forma's six floors to lobbies. The lobby levels, which alternate with floors of guestrooms, are open and public, and can be shaped into different stage configurations. A hydraulic platform interconnects the levels and provides even more flexibility. Two of the lobbies have large, open-air arcades facing Ørestad City's public square.

Theatrical interactions are also built into the architecture and programming of the guestroom floors. Spaces can be easily customized into hotel rooms, dressing rooms, and/or studios, via plug-in modular units. Each unit—ordered like room service in traditional hotels—provides a particular amenity, such as a bed, dressing counter, or editing suite.

In designing the Hotel Pro Forma fieldOFFICE and nARCHITECTS were inspired by a tour of New York's Waldorf-Astoria Hotel, which revealed the building's complex overlap of private and public functions, from hotel rooms, apartments, and ballrooms to offices. (The architect Rem Koolhaas reproduced a famous 1937 cutaway drawing of the hotel as a symbol of urban density in his 1978 "retroactive manifesto," *Delirious New York*.) The Hotel Pro Forma revives this image of the urban hotel not only as a jewel in the city, but as a dynamic city itself.

—E.J.

Like New York's Waldorf-Astoria Hotel, which functions as a city-within-the-city, the proposed Hotel Pro Forma (top) combines hotel, theater, and exhibition space in a series of flexible, multipurpose spaces. Lobbies (below left and middle) occur on every other floor and accommodate typical hotel functions such as reception, check-in, bookstores, and bars as well as rehearsal and performance spaces. Guests configure their own rooms (below right) by ordering plug-in modular units via an expanded definition of room service.

THE NEW LAS VEGAS

Photographs by Richard Barnes

Although cities from Singapore to London boast great hotels, no city is so clearly identified with the hotel as Las Vegas. Originally a gambling and drinking center for workers building the nearby Hoover Dam in the 1930s, Las Vegas came into its own after World War II. Hotels were first built downtown, but they soon spread south, creating what has come to be called the Strip with Bugsy Siegel's Flamingo, the Frontier, Stardust, and, in 1966, Caesars Palace. The last became an icon of architecture as stage set, complete with Cleopatra's Bar floating in water, staff in "Roman" costumes, and reproductions of Classical statuary.

Richard Barnes's photographs, specially commissioned for this book, illuminate a new Las Vegas. Over the last thirty years families and convention-goers have become the most common visitors, and, concurrently, gambling has lost its position as the number-one activity; it is now less popular than entertainment, dining, and shopping. These changes have affected the architecture of local hotels in two ways: hotels have become much larger and even more entertainment-driven in their stylistic excess.

Contemporary Las Vegas is not only a city of hotels; it is a city of hotels that mimic other cities. Time and space seem to collapse where the Eiffel Tower is just up the street from St. Mark's Square, Egyptian pyramids, and the Empire State Building. Icons of Paris, Venice, Bellagio, Luxor, and New York are pieced together into architectural collages. Each hotel's theme is developed in built form and then carried through to staff uniforms, restaurant cuisine, souvenirs, and signage. The illusionism extends to landscaping as well. Pools, fountains, grassy lawns, and golf courses mask the fact that Las Vegas is surrounded by desert. These themed hotels are urbanizing Las Vegas itself with outdoor civic spaces. Today its sidewalks are jammed with tourists, and bridges over busy thoroughfares allow pedestrian access to hotels.

Richard Barnes's photographs are not so much documentary as highly interpretive views of contemporary Las Vegas. In contrast to the cheerful vistas of casinos in travel brochures, Barnes's pictures emphasize Las Vegas as an illusion by taking the viewer behind the scenes to see the city's infrastructure—acres of unpopulated garages, concrete parking lots, and barren construction sites that support its entertainment industry. He flattens Las Vegas's scenographic excess—made all the more shadowless by the mercilessly bright sky over the desert. He also revels in the knife-sharp edge between the desert and the city and between the fake and the real, exposing the thinness of the illusion that covers the city's rampant commercial impulse.

—D.A.

Richard Barnes's photo essay includes images of such new Las Vegas hotels as the pyramid-shaped Luxor (left) and the Venetian (pages 63–65). Las Vegas now contains 125,000 hotel rooms, more than any other American city.

URBAN HOTELS

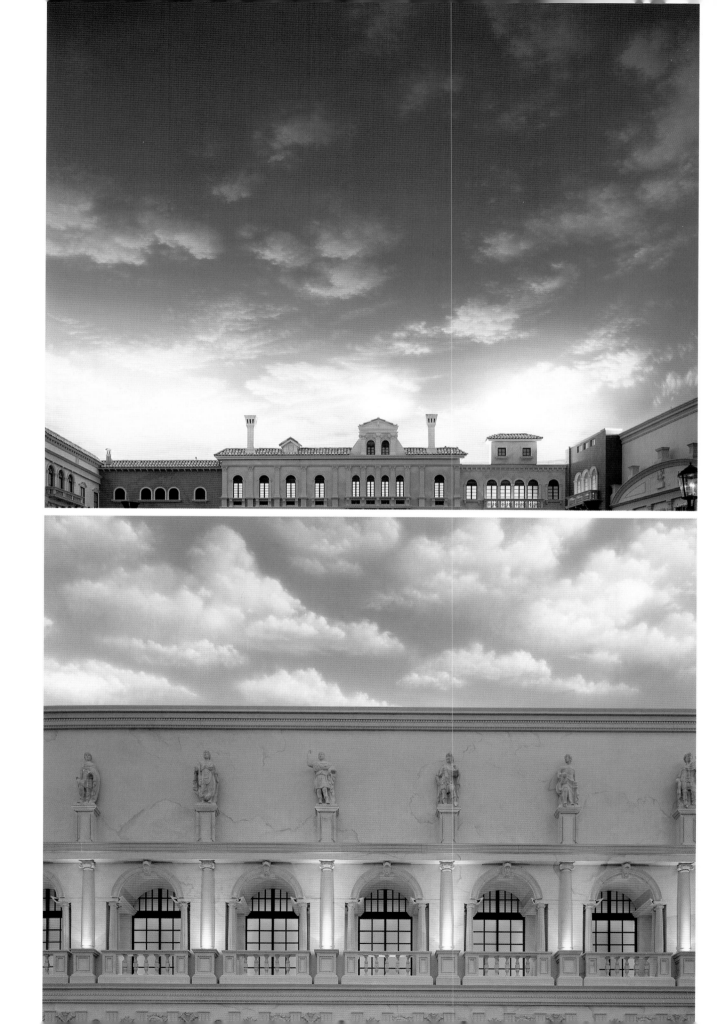

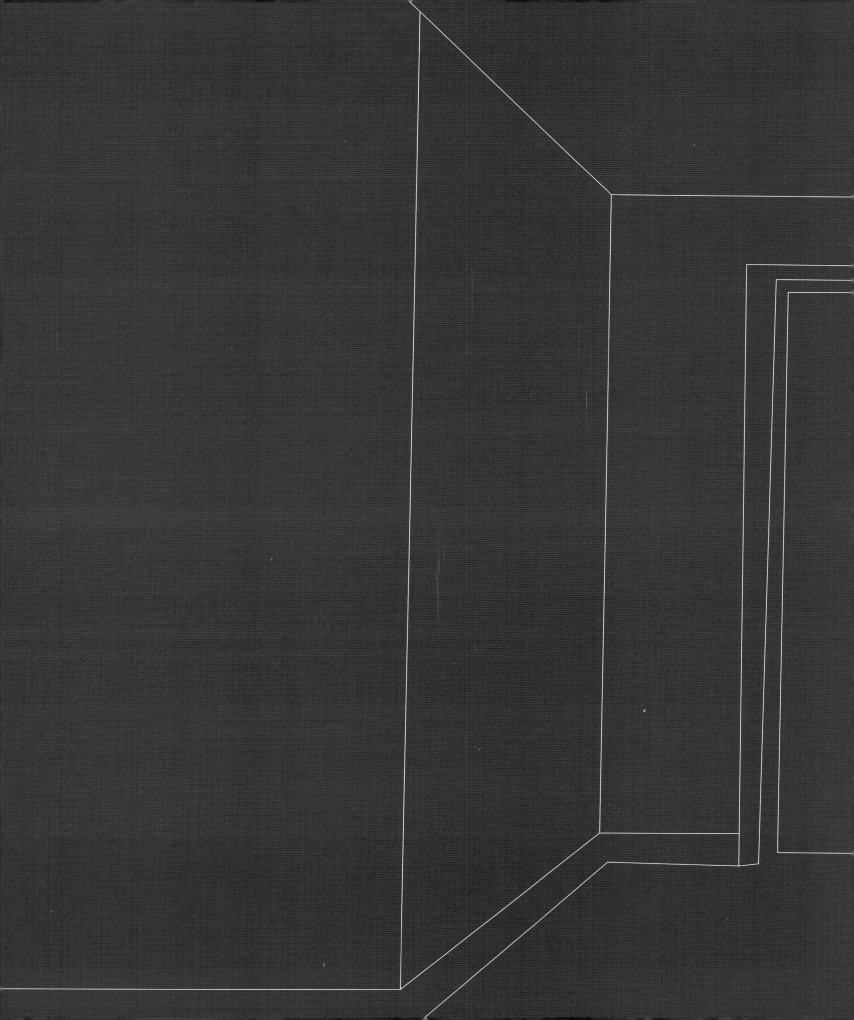

619

HOTELS ON THE MOVE

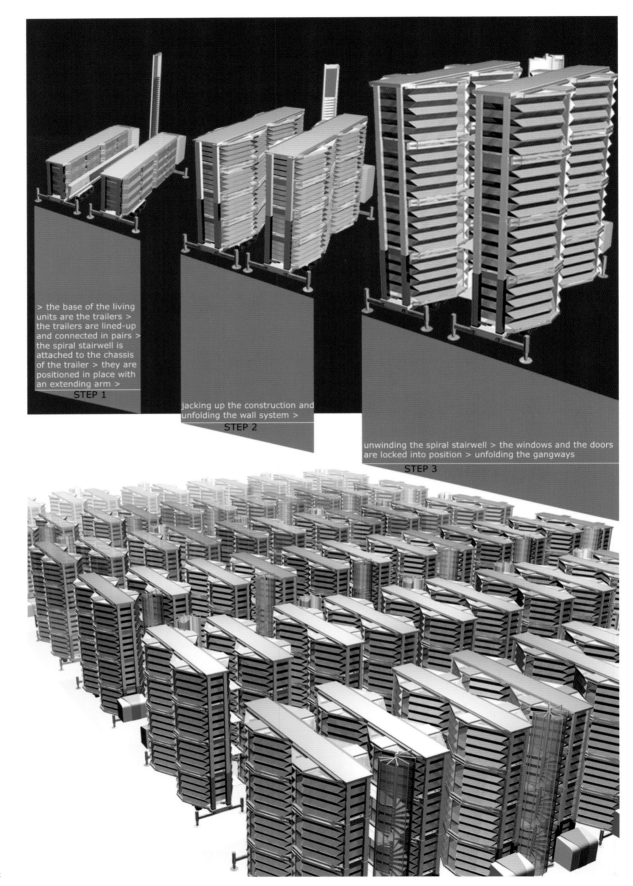

> the base of the living units are the trailers > the trailers are lined-up and connected in pairs > the spiral stairwell is attached to the chassis of the trailer > they are positioned in place with an extending arm >
STEP 1

jacking up the construction and unfolding the wall system >
STEP 2

unwinding the spiral stairwell > the windows and the doors are locked into position > unfolding the gangways
STEP 3

LIVING UNITS IN MOTION

Carl de Smet / Uncontrollable Architectural Products

"A changing society," says Belgian-born Carl de Smet of Uncontrollable Architectural Products, "constantly puts forward new and different demands." Issues of flexibility, adaptability, and mobility inform all of this designer's work—from a pocket-sized coffeemaker to such full-scale building systems as Living Units in Motion, which examine these issues in relation to hotels. Addressing both cultural and ecological needs, Living Units accommodate large numbers of people for short periods, for example during international trade shows, Olympic Games, and even natural disasters. They are also recyclable and leave only a minimal, temporary footprint on their sites.

Inspired by such figures as R. Buckminster Fuller and the postwar British architecture group Archigram as well as emerging technologies, Uncontrollable Architectural Products combines architecture and transportation. De Smet's modular Living Units are mounted onto standard European tractor trailers. While in transit, each unit, including platform floors and sailcloth walls, is compressed like a collapsed accordion. It then easily opens into a four-story structure through the use of hydraulic jacks at the site, with the trailer now functioning as the foundation. The platforms and walls are designed so that when compressed they form a rectangle that fits the trailer's plan, but when unfolded become a more spacious octagon. For structural stability and circulation, each Living Unit requires a minimum of two trailers side by side; gangway corridors and a spiral stairwell fit into the space between. Each trailer has two living units per floor, thus the minimum Living Unit hotel houses sixteen rooms. This configuration can be installed by four people in only one hour.

The Living Unit design incorporates all modern conveniences. Each trailer has its own mechanical room with laundry facilities and electrical generator. An external reservoir attached to the outside of the unit stores a week's supply of water. All of the rooms are designed with furnishings adapted to the collapsible structure: a foldaway double bed, a toilet with an unfoldable enclosure, and a shower with a telescopic basin.

Linked to military and exploratory campaigns, mobile housing—from tents to Quonset huts—has a long history. In more recent times, people have used tents and small trailers for camping in remote places. Uncontrollable Architectural Products applies this tradition on a new, larger scale, bringing modern industry and corporate size to contemporary travel.

—D.A.

Living Units in Motion, which are shipped on truck beds, expand like accordions to form hotels serving large numbers of people for such short-term gatherings as trade shows and sporting events.

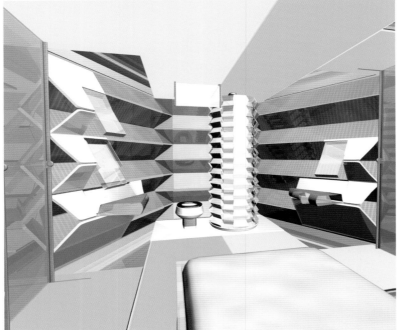

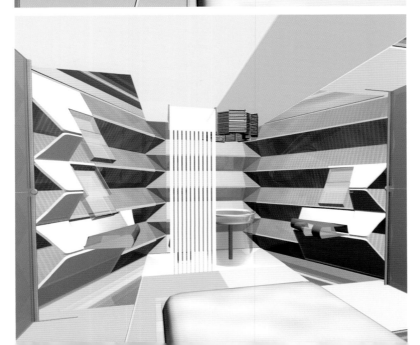

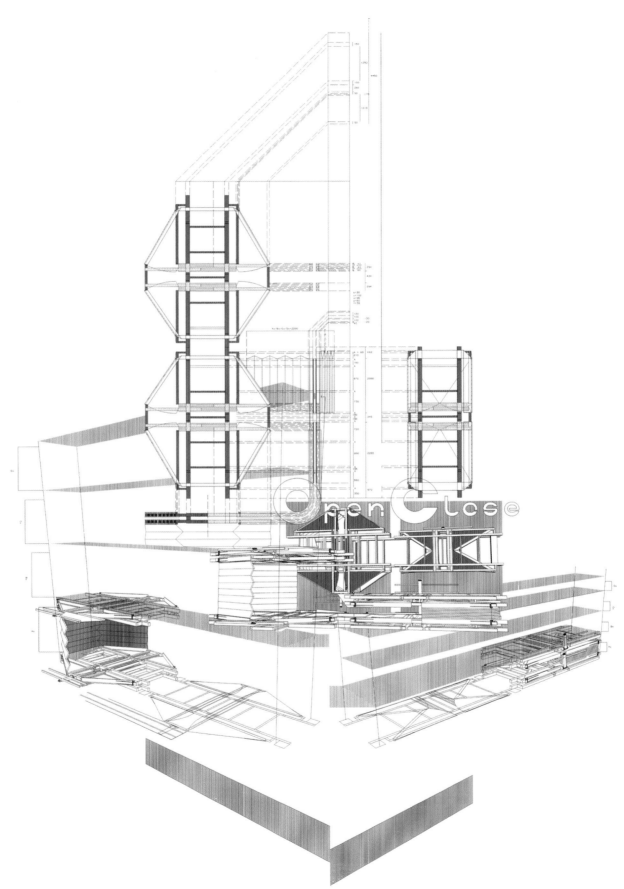

Acconci Studio

JAPANESE CAR HOTEL

1995

Cars have long symbolized personal mobility and recently have come to represent personal space, particularly to people who endure long commutes. The transformation of a car into a mobile capsule hotel takes these attributes one step further. Vito Acconci, the noted performance artist, founded the architectural firm Acconci Studio in 1990 to design public spaces, furniture, and vehicles. "It's important to me that my work is in the public realm, and that it's useful," Acconci states.

In the Japanese Car Hotel, modeled but never built, a conventional car is converted from a carriage for passengers to a temporary resting space. The car remains driveable, with an unaltered engine and driver's seat, but the rest of the interior is filled with four stackable bed-and-seat units, attached to a hydraulic piston. In the trunk is a hydraulic pump. The upper

body—roof and sides—of the car lifts hydraulically off the base to serve as the roof of a four-story mini-hotel, as bed units also separate and rise. Each rubber bed consists of a pillow at one end and a seat at the other. A television mounted next to the seat is directed toward the bed below. The units are joined by a chain ladder.

Although the Car Hotel could be built using many brands of automobiles, Acconci has designated the project "Japanese"—in reference, perhaps, to the modularity of traditional Japanese construction (from tatami mats to today's capsule hotels), to the country's innovative automobile industry, or to the way the Car Hotel unfolds like a piece of origami.

—E.J.

Acconci Studio has developed a design for converting a car into a hotel with four stacked and expandable bed-and-seat units.

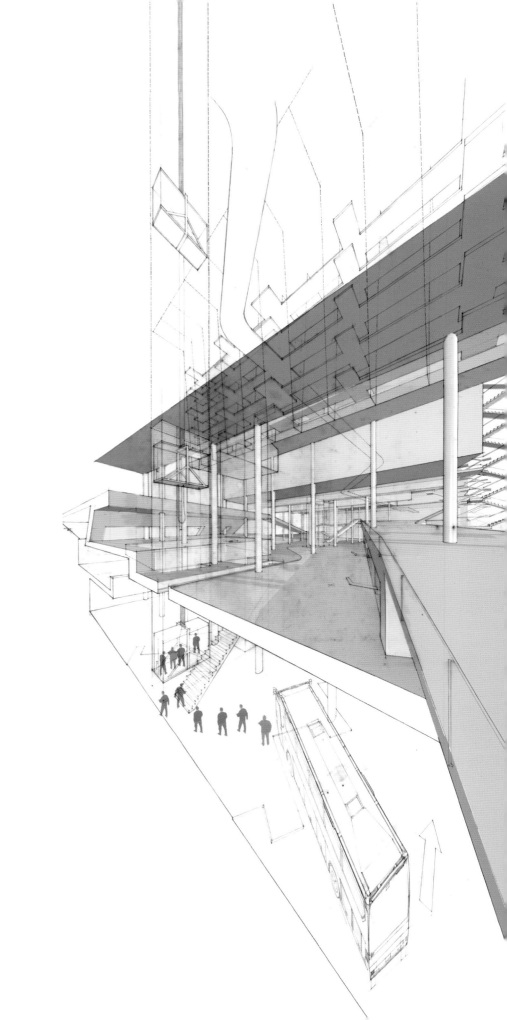

HOTELS ON THE MOVE

Lewis.Tsurumaki.Lewis

TOURBUS HOTEL

ROME, ITALY 2002

For centuries Rome has been one of the most popular tourist destinations in the world. The annual number of tourists reached a peak of 30,000,000 in the jubilee year of 2000, up about 10% from previous years. Today travelers arrive by plane, train, and—more and more frequently—tourbus. Chartered bus tours are now one of the most rapidly expanding segments of the tourism industry, packaging small groups of like-minded customers who visit preselected sites, eat preselected meals, and lodge at preselected hotels. Given that tours can be put together for as few as ten people per bus (although average tours are thirty to fourty-four people per bus), the range of specialized tours is vast: for example, doctors study art from an anatomical perspective, epicureans sample regional cuisines, and women worship at goddess sites. The tourbus is both a mobile social condenser and a lens through which the city is viewed.

When architect Paul Lewis, a partner in the New York firm Lewis.Tsurumaki.Lewis, was studying at the American Academy in Rome in the late 1990s, he was struck by the overwhelming presence of tourbuses in the center of the city. Using congestion as the catalyst and the tourbus as the module, he developed a new building type: the Tourbus Hotel. This concept, recently expanded upon by the firm, facilitates tourism by the busload. Registration, in an underground parking garage, assigns each busload to its own floor of the hotel. The layout of each floor reinforces the communal space of the bus, with the aisle becoming the corridor and the seats relating to the rooms. Even when guests retreat to their private hotel rooms, the public nature of the bus follows them, as the corridor is lined with monitors that display the television programs guests are watching.

In order to accommodate the variety of bus tours available, Lewis.Tsurumaki.Lewis designed their hotel as an aggregate of ten mini-hotels, reflecting the range of service, style, and price from youth hostels to two-star hotels. Connected by glass corridors, these mini-hotels share a large, skylit lobby that is open to the street and adjoins the surrounding Porta Portese neighborhood, including its famous Sunday flea market on the banks of the River Tiber. A water taxi line shuttles guests to central Rome, offering easy access to the most popular local sites while revital-izing an underused section of the city. The lobby and water taxi promote the possibility of limited exchanges with travelers from other bus groups.

As a physical environment, however, the hotel primarily reinforces the connections between individual travelers and their small, temporary group, amplifying its insularity. Lewis.Tsurumaki.Lewis's project extends the protective sheath of the tourbus to the hotel experience.

—E.J.

Registration at the Tourbus Hotel occurs by busload in the underground parking garage. The lobby opens onto the active street.

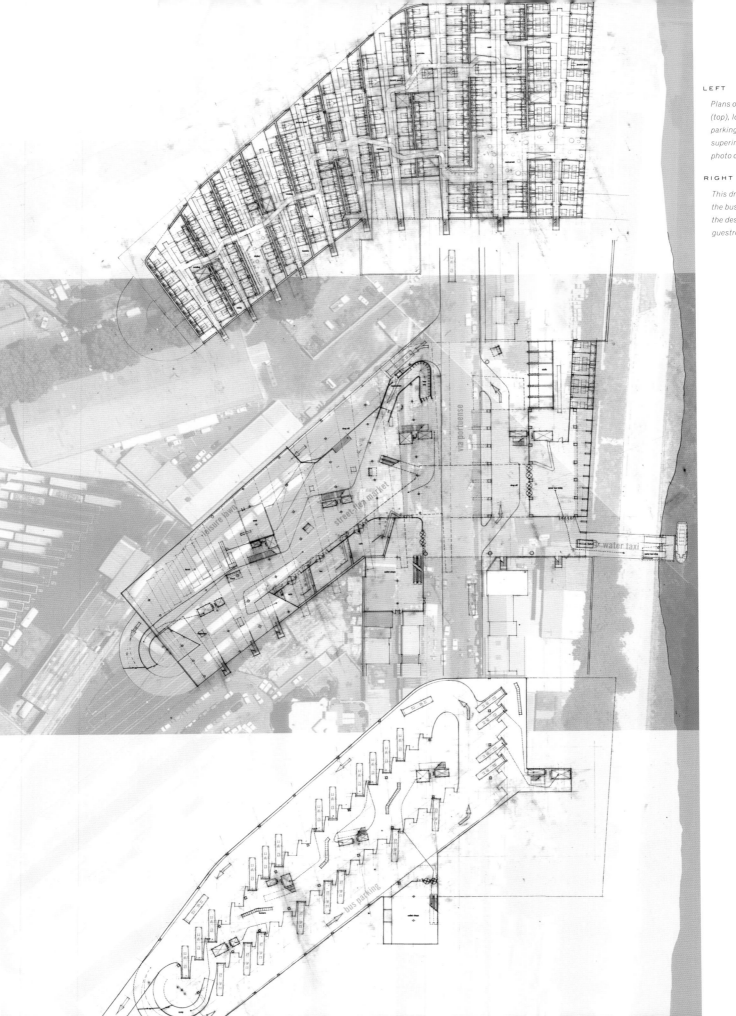

leisure lawn

street-flea market

via portuense

water taxi

bus parking

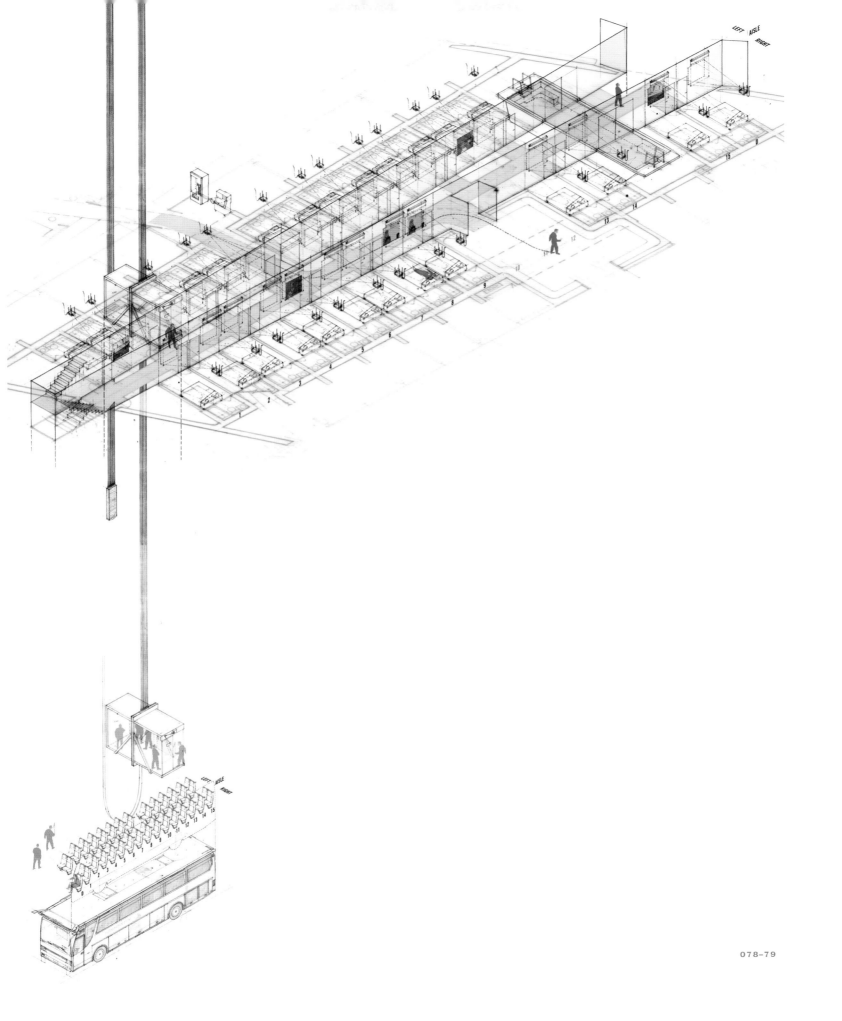

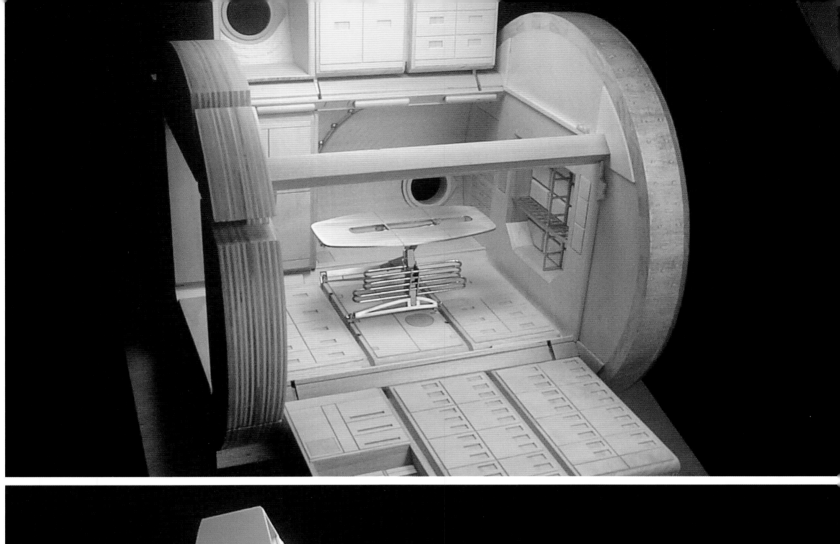

Habitability Design Center, Johnson Space Center

HABITATION MODULE

INTERNATIONAL SPACE STATION 2001

In the 1920s, when architect Le Corbusier described the house as a "machine for living," he probably couldn't have imagined the extreme functional requirements of designing for domestic life in space. But as astronauts' missions have expanded from a day or two to many months, the architects of the Habitability Design Center (HDC) have begun to design a personal module for NASA that addresses, in the words of Garrett Finney, HDC's lead architect, "not just what it takes to survive the experience of being in space, but to live there."

Eventually NASA's Habitation Module will be the residence capsule of the International Space Station. Although designed as temporary quarters for scientists, the module is presented here as a sophisticated template for a comfortable space hotel that could serve the nascent space tourism market. The Module is far from a Four Seasons hotel, but it successfully allows for human comfort in a thoroughly inhospitable environment.

The entire module, which houses six people, is just 8.5 m (28 ft) long and 4.5 m (15 ft) in diameter. Most elements of the module will be launched as separate parts to save space and then assembled once in orbit. Despite its extremely small size, each module contains a pullout galley kitchen, a collapsible table for meals and meetings, and private quarters for the rotating crew. The private quarters are furnished with a sleeping restraint, a desk, communications outlets, lighting and ventilation, and—most radically—a wall of Velcro and bungee cords for displaying personal effects.

The new design represents a quantum leap forward for space habitation standards, which since the 1970s have forced astronauts to sleep in bunks with virtually no privacy, in morgue-like drawers, or in sleeping bags hanging along public corridors. But after the near disasters aboard Mir, the 1990s space station where tours of duty lasted two weeks to fourteen months, NASA recognized that the lack of privacy and basic human comforts contributed to flaring tempers and bad science. Dr. Al Holland, NASA's chief of psychology, notes, "We've learned that if you put bright, active people in a socially and sensory tedious environment, they're going to get the blahs or worse."

To make the Habitation Module an environment in which people could live, the architects of the HDC considered every element. Without the force of gravity, even opening a cupboard or turning a dial necessitates a grip for leverage, and every gathering space requires extra design attention. The communal table has no chairs around it because sitting in zero-gravity space is difficult. Instead, footholds under the table allow the astronauts to "moor" themselves, and the same principle is applied to the "beds" in the private quarters. The table has a special suction system to collect crumbs before they become airborne and a trough in the center to circulate air. With no natural air movement in space, the exhalations of the small group of astronauts could create enough carbon dioxide to suffocate them.

Aesthetic issues are more resistant to change. The modules need to remain largely monochromatic because colors on the space station convey important messages, such as where to find emergency supplies and which direction is up, making decorative color potentially dangerous. The visual monotony of white is relieved, however, by a narrow palette of light colors that Finney dubs "military pastels."

Earlier accommodations for astronauts have been designed by engineers only; the Habitation Module is the first to be created with architects as part of the team. "Architects at NASA are becoming bigger players," said Kriss Kennedy, a NASA architect. "We're the ones who put the living back in living in space." —E.J.

While the Habitation Module has been designed for the International Space Station, it is also a prototypical hotel for tourism in outer space.

080–81

The proposed Lunatic Hotel is designed as a pair of slender towers with capsules that can house approximately two hundred tourists on the moon.

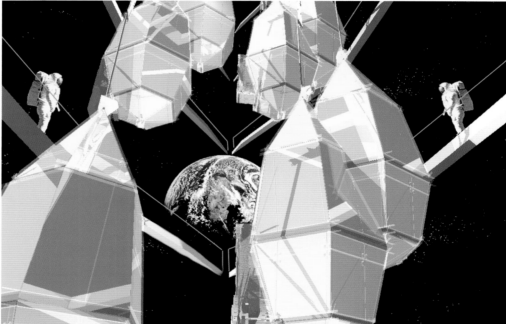

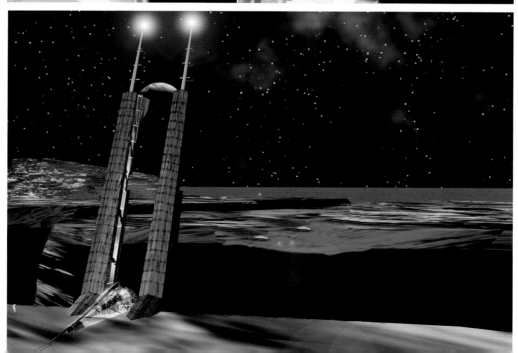

Hans-Jurgen Rombaut

LUNATIC HOTEL

2000

Tourism to the "final frontier" became a reality in 2001 when American businessman Dennis Tito paid Russia $20,000,000 to send him to the International Space Station. Although the station had room for one extra guest, the prospect of space tourism on a larger scale requires a new kind of hotel. Dutch architect Hans-Jurgen Rombaut has designed the Lunatic Hotel, which he calls a "sensation engine," to accommodate travelers to the moon. It is not the first proposal for lunar lodging, but some science writers believe it to be the most advanced and technically feasible.

The Lunatic Hotel would be built with materials culled from the moon's surface to avoid the expense of transporting building materials from Earth. Rombaut's design shields his guests from the harsh lunar environment, where radiation is lethal, temperatures range from 120 to –160 degrees Celsius, and the ultra-thin atmosphere makes it impossible to breathe. The hotel walls are 50 cm (20 in) thick moon rock. Water is held between the windows' two glass panes to help stabilize the temperature within the structure. Some of the moon's unusual environmental conditions actually facilitate the architecture of the Lunatic Hotel. The hotel's two slender, tapering towers, each 160 m (500 ft) high, would be easier to engineer and build on the moon because of its low gravity and lack of wind. In fact the low gravity means that the thick exterior wall would weigh less than a 7 cm (2.75 in) thick concrete wall on Earth.

The design, Rombaut's Masters thesis at the Rotterdam Academy of Architecture, has a glass-covered reception area at its center. From the towers flanking this structure, guests see the Earth. The guestrooms, or "habitation capsules," for about two hundred tourists hang from slender beams in the towers. They are shaped like small spaceships in order to make guests feel as though they are still traveling through space. Each unit has an air-lock entrance and waste and water facilities. Rooms for the hotel's staff—who would live on site and be exposed to the dangerous environment for much longer periods than guests—are underground. All meals are eaten within the hotel, so the design includes a variety of restaurants, bars, and lounges. Entertainment spaces provide for moon-specific activities, from indoor mountaineering to "flying courts." Indeed, the low gravity (one-sixth of the Earth's) could cause muscle deterioration, even over a brief stay. Elevators and "atmospheric" or "vacuum" passages would provide easy circulation, but guests would be encouraged to walk to the top of the towers.

"The most recent knowledge about the moon has been taken into account" in Rombaut's design, says Bernard Foing at the European Space Research and Technology Centre in The Netherlands. Foing is also chair of the Lunar Explorers Society, whose goal is to construct a lunar village by 2040. "This hotel would fit very well in our scheme," he says. Rombaut's level of rigor in solving the real problems of building and living on the moon underscores the feasibility of space tourism in the near future, as it moves beyond the realm of military projects and science fiction.

—E.J.

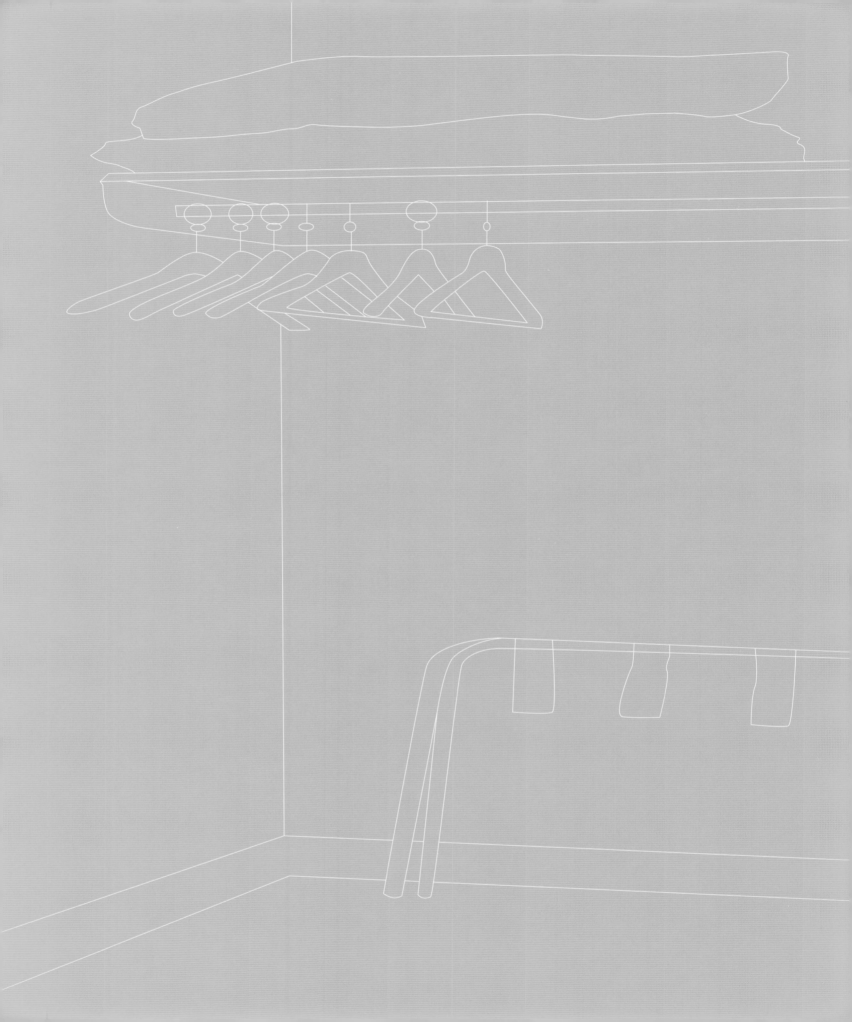

HOTELS AS GLOBAL BUSINESS

24/7 HOTEL ROOM

Joel Sanders Architect

In the hotel, which serves as a "home away from home," today's business travelers require the same kind of multifunctional spaces that people increasingly demand from their dwellings: flexible environments that accommodate both domestic and professional activities. In addition to beds and bathrooms, guests want wired workstations with high-speed Internet access and seating areas where they can conduct meetings with colleagues and clients. Joel Sanders's 24/7 Hotel Room, specially commissioned for New Hotels for Global Nomads, fits the size of a conventional business-hotel room (3.6 x 7.4 m [12 x 24 ft]), but reconfigures its layout and furniture to provide a new kind of fluid environment to meet these new needs.

The 24/7 Hotel Room dissolves the boundaries between work and leisure. Rather than separate the space's home and office functions into discrete areas, Sanders conceived the 24/7 Hotel Room as an open, multi-purpose landscape. Each prefabricated unit is made up of an exterior fiber-glass shell housing two rooms that can be opened into one large suite. The shell is molded into undulating forms to create four zones within each room—an office/seating area, a bed/conversation pit, a spa/bathroom, and a fitness center. Sheathed in continuous, durable, commercial-grade upholstery, the zones are defined by changes in floor level. In addition, translucent partitions that double as projection screens electronically roll down from the ceiling to divide the areas for privacy. Storage, which runs from window to corridor and services all four zones, is integrated into the folded membrane of the fiberglass wall. Sanders has also transformed the corridor of a typical hotel from a narrow circulation spine into a vital new social space. Its length is activated by lounges and conference areas and overlooks a skylit central atrium. Blending public and private spaces, the guestrooms open on to the corridor via a retractable wall.

The 24/7 Hotel Room collapses hard and fast distinctions between building scale and human scale. It fuses architecture and furniture, offering an environment molded to the personal and professional needs of the global business traveler.   —D.A.

24/7 Hotel Room units, with projecting individual fitness centers, can be combined to make up a conventional-sized hotel.

*The 24|7 Hotel Room is an
open, multipurpose landscape
of different work and leisure
functions tailored to contemporary business travel. Each
prefabricated fiberglass unit
contains two rooms.*

BELOW

*Cutaway of 24|7 Hotel Room
showing the rolldown screens
that can subdivide the space
and the mechanical system
below the floor.*

RIGHT

*Bathroom, spa, and conversa-
tion pit can be left open or
divided with rolldown screens.
The double-wide module is
shown open.*

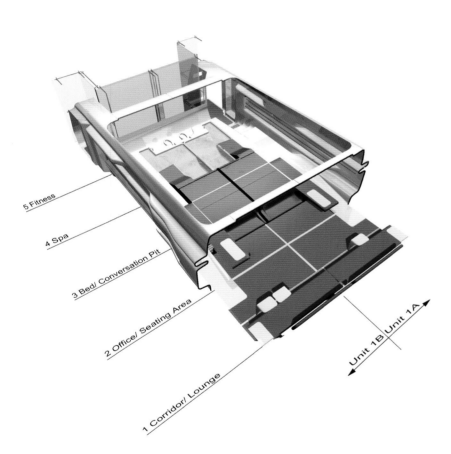

5 Fitness

4 Spa

3 Bed/ Conversation Pit

2 Office/ Seating Area

1 Corridor/ Lounge

Unit 1B | Unit 1A

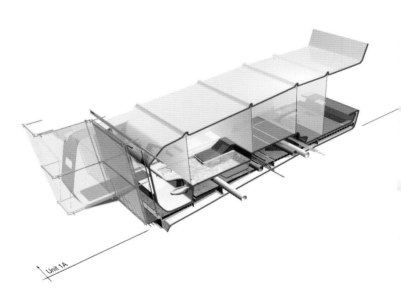

Unit 1A

SPIRITUALITY

SHOES A LEXICON OF STYLE

BEAUTIFUL THINGS

John Rair

Rockwell Group

W HOTELS

1998–PRESENT

W Hotels, owned by Starwood Hotels & Resorts—the largest hotel company in the United States, whose chains include Sheraton and Westin—dress the business hotel in an intimate boutique hotel's clothing. Health and wellness, rather than the typical boutique's sex and glitz, are the keys to the Rockwell Group's designs in developing this new brand.

The first to open, in 1998, was the 720-room W New York, across the street from the venerable Waldorf-Astoria Hotel; it was followed by, at present, fifteen branches in ten cities. Although not all its hotels were designed by the Rockwell Group, the chain uses the naturalistic template created by them. As conceived by Starwood chairman and CEO Barry Sternlicht, the W brand appeals to young, affluent business travelers and, in its high-style bars and restaurant, fashionable locals. As one of his business models Sternlicht points to the success of Starbucks in creating a new market niche for a traditional product by putting it in a great package.

Rockwell's answer to Sternlicht's brief was, according to architect David Rockwell, "to establish not a 'traditional-luxury' hotel, not a 'nightclub-scene' boutique hotel, not a 'domestic' home away from home, but an urban oasis designed for rejuvenation." In addition to the high-tech conference facilities and ballrooms standard in business hotels, the first W includes a large, full-service spa that offers organic treatments. Rockwell recalls that the hotel was designed "from the spa outward."

The four elements—fire, air, earth, and water—inform the design at every level. While checking in at a desk decorated with potted herbs, each guest is offered a glass of juice. The lobby is painted in earth tones and furnished in part with cocktail tables, some of which look like tree trunks and others that are topped with crushed sunflower seeds. This aesthetic blueprint is followed at subsequent branches. At New York's W Union Square, also designed by Rockwell, the lobby's grand staircase is trimmed with grass, and the walls are covered in dense ivy. Visitors to the W Times Square, designed by Toronto-based Yabu Pushelberg, enter the complex through a vestibule of waterfalls. At the W New York visitors can return the favor that nature provides throughout the rest of the hotel. On the guestroom windowsills are a copper watering can and a planter of wheatgrass that beckons "Water me!"   —D.A.

The W Hotel uses elements of nature to brand this business chain as more of a restorative spa than a "nightclub-scene hotel." The lobby of the W Hotel Union Square features a plant wall and a palette of earthtones.

The bed is the focal point of the guestrooms in the W New York. Its down comforter is bordered with soothing phrases like "sleep with angels" (top). Mini-lawns grow in stone benches at the W New York (middle). Restaurants and bars in the W Hotels are meant to attract local residents as well as hotel guests. Columns in the Heart-break restaurant at the W New York are clad in jeweled mosaics (bottom).

OPPOSITE

Water surrounds visitors entering the W Times Square.

Spike Jonze/director and Fatboy Slim/musical artist

"WEAPON OF CHOICE"

2001

In order to express the rejuvenating power of music, director Spike Jonze and his editor, Eric Zumbrunnen, selected a prosaic Marriott hotel in downtown Los Angeles as the unexpected setting for their award-winning music video "Weapon of Choice." The video opens with a modern-day Willy Loman, played by dancer-turned-actor Christopher Walken, slumped over his luggage in the hotel's lobby after a long day on the road. From a nearby radio comes Fatboy Slim's rhythmic music, a witty reversal of the corporate Muzak that permeates offices, hotels, and airports. Walken suddenly perks up: he can't stop himself from dancing and cartwheeling through the hotel's atrium and up its escalator, and finally diving from a balcony to hover weightlessly above the banal surroundings. The inhuman quality of the hotel is exaggerated by the total absence of other people. Fatboy Slim (also known as Norman Cook) hopes his songs, which remix a variety of music and "found" sounds, will make listeners "start doing uncontrollable dancing." In the "Weapon of Choice" video he's so successful that even in the most inhospitable environment a worn-out salesman can't suppress the urge to dance.

—D.A.

Diller + Scofidio

INTERCLONE HOTEL

1997

Elizabeth Diller and Ricardo Scofidio's InterClone Hotel comments ironically on the sameness of many international chain hotels and is an acerbic critique of globalization. Seeking to put theoretical ideas about culture into practice, this New York–based husband-and-wife team created the project for the 1997 Istanbul Biennial, for which it was displayed as a series of advertisements along the concourse of the local airport. To heighten the satiric impact, the images were interspersed with the airport's real advertisements of similarly marketed global brands.

The fictional InterClone Hotel is a chain in six pilot cities—from Tijuana, Mexico, to Ho Chi Minh City, Vietnam—where globalization and emerging economies are, in the words of the architects, "erasing distinctions between 'third world' and 'first world.'" Although these erasures create a monolithic world culture, Diller + Scofidio note that "tourism retroactively fabricates diversity for its own sustenance." In their project, a thin veneer of decor inspired by local culture serves this need of worldwide tourism. Surfaces—wallpaper, bedspreads, and carpet—are varied, while the room's layout—Western-style double bed, bureau, lamps, and television—remain constant. Even the room's links to the outside world—the view through the plate-glass window and on the television—portray a deadening homogeneity. Each country's rich natural and cultural history has been reduced to flat motifs, for example a zebra-patterned rug that connotes the wildlife of Uganda. The wallpaper patterns—computers, factories, oil drills, and so on—represent the high-tech future.

The advertisement for each hotel in the chain is further coded with a menu of information that the architects consider essential for the tourist. The number of kilometers from the hotel to the local airport lets guests know how quickly they can escape if a revolution occurs. The city's growth index and labor base inform business travelers of the state of its economy. Finally, Diller + Scofidio warn of the chief regional hazard, from potholes to kidnappings, acknowledging the local dangers in rapidly changing cities swept up in global tourism.

—D.A.

As depicted in these mock advertisements, the fictional InterClone Hotel critiques the superficially local decor in otherwise homogeneous international chain hotels.

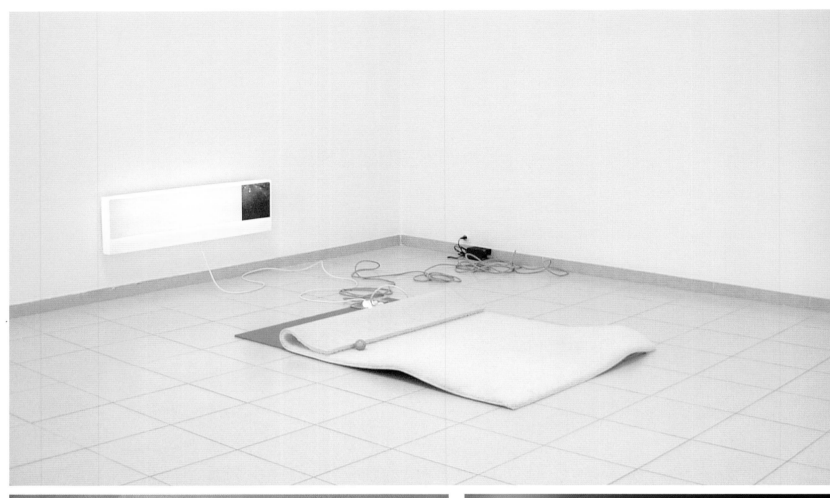

Dike Blair

"#1289, SEEKONK, MA"

2002

Through painting and sculpture, Dike Blair subverts the homogeneity of American chain motels. Unmade beds, empty pools, and dirty ashtrays are sensuously rendered in gouache. His sculptures use the materials of the generic corporate interior—carpet, fluorescent lighting, and electrical cords—to create abstractions of guestrooms from the low end of the hospitality market. This duality between the handmade and the factory-produced, the warm and the cool, expresses Blair's ambivalence toward modern rootlessness and consumerism. "When I set out I am simply looking for what in the world attracts me," Blair says. "That involves a camera and looking for places that I find pleasing or troubling or poignant or whatever." Blair's gouaches recall the soft-edged melancholy of Edward Hopper, while his sculptures evoke the 1970s minimalism of Dan Flavin and Robert Morris.

Blair addresses the way in which corporate culture and global tourism have commodified nature by framing it as a spectacle seen through the windows of cars, planes, and hotels. "As more and more of nature is given over to culture," Blair says, "the geometries of the carpet start to resemble cultivated landscapes." The rooms in his gouaches are often decorated with forgettable landscape paintings, such as the seascape hanging above the bed in his 1999 *Untitled*. The fluorescent screen in the sculpture *Tile Field* displays a photograph of a green lawn with a flock of white birds.

#1289, Seekonk, MA, created specifically for *New Hotels for Global Nomads*, is Blair's abstract response to a Motel 6 in a small town in Massachusetts. An untraditional form of sculpture, the work uses light and color to evoke the motel room's emotional ambience.

The artist's use of hotels as inspiration for his work is a logical extension of his interest in the pervasiveness of buildings serving today's leisure and entertainment culture. Other Blair projects have focused on Disney World's Epcot Center, strip clubs, airport lounges, and bars. In his work Blair celebrates and helps people see the beauty and value of the overlooked. "Maybe the guys painting parking slot lines or installing acoustic ceiling tiles aren't aware of the extraordinary beauty of the pattern," he has noted. "That's where the artist comes in."

—D.A.

Dike Blair's sculptures and gouaches such as Tile Field *(top) and* Untitled *(bottom left), depict the furniture, carpet, fluorescent lighting, and electrical cords of generic roadside motels.*
A new work entitled #1289, Seekonk, MA, *created for* New Hotels for Global Nomads, *has been inspired by a motel room in the eponymous Massachusetts town (bottom right).*

Kotobuki Company

CAPSULE HOTEL UNITS <small>2001</small>
<small>2002</small> # "CAPSULE HOTEL"

Jeff Gompertz, fakeshop

Capsule hotels were developed in Japan in the late 1970s as a response to sudden increases in population, urban density, workdays, and business commutes. These small, urban hotels offer businesspeople and other travelers extremely compact sleeping compartments at a modest price. They combine small guestrooms with larger public spaces and amenities—from bars, lounges, and restaurants to spas, gyms, and mah-jongg rooms. The fiberglass capsules are 90 x 180 x 100 cm (35.5 x 71 x 39 in); a television and an alarm clock are embedded in the shell. The capsules are still manufactured today by Kotobuki, which supplied the units for the first Capsule Inn, built in Osaka in 1977.

Capsule hotels relate to various elements of Japanese culture. They continue the national tradition of modular construction and building parts. In fact, the dimensions of the capsule's plan exactly match those of the tatami mat. More recent precedents include the Metabolist architecture movement of the 1960s, whose proponents sought to bring the newly expanded urbanized city into harmony with nature. Small, prefabricated capsules that could be quickly added to or subtracted from buildings made the city more responsive to rapid change. The first realization of these concepts was architect Kisho Kurokawa's Nagakin Capsule Building of 1972, in Tokyo, which featured fully outfitted, prefabricated, small (2.5 x 3.6 m [8 x 12 ft]), living units.

Of the various modular buildings, however, capsule hotels in particular have captured the public imagination. Science-fiction writer William Gibson, who coined the term "cyberspace," sets part of the opening of his 1984 book *Neuromancer* in a capsule hotel. Gibson connected the hotel to the incipient Internet, a link that has inspired New York–based artist Jeff Gompertz. Gompertz, a partner in the art and media collective Fakeshop, stayed in a capsule hotel in Tokyo and decided to build his own full-scale version.

In Gompertz's first *Capsule Hotel*, built in 1999, each module—in addition to functioning as a hotel room—was outfitted with its own camera and television, making it a "channel" capable of transmitting and receiving signals from all other channels, or capsules, in the system. Sixty-two capsules served as short-term housing for approximately seventy people. The compartmental nature of the hotel's physical structure deliberately paralleled the workings of an Internet chat room. In a second version, from May 2001, a computer with video conferencing capabilities was included in each capsule and allows transmission beyond the hotel. No longer a closed-circuit system, *Capsule Hotel* became accessible to remote users via an Internet connection.

Isolation and connectedness, private and public—while characteristic of all hotels, these themes are especially evident in the capsule hotel. The underlying voyeuristic appeal of Gompertz's installation is also present in the original Japanese hotels, whose doors are not solid, so guests can hear one another's activities within their rooms. In a case of life following art, the low levels of privacy and anonymity in the Japanese capsule hotels are now seen as one of their primary attractions.

—E.J.

Gompertz's Capsule Hotel *was inspired by his stay in a Tokyo capsule hotel.*

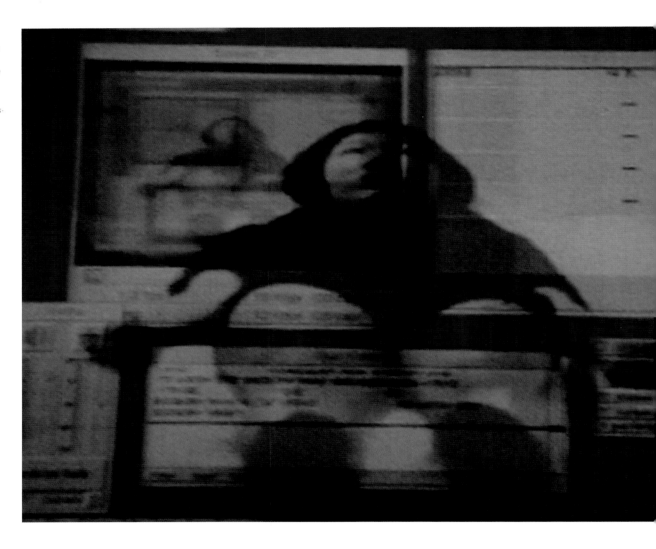

In a video Gompertz made of his Capsule Hotel *installation*, a dancer thoroughly explores the units. Gompertz outfits the units with cameras and television, making each capsule its own "channel" capable of transmitting and receiving signals from all other channels, or capsules, in the system.

STANDARD, HOLLYWOOD Shawn Hausman

Koning Eizenberg and Shawn Hausman

STANDARD, DOWNTOWN L.A. 2002

2002 (PROPOSED)

STANDARD, NEW YORK Gluckman Mayner Architects

"The Standard," owner and hotelier André Balazs says, "is anything but." With aesthetically unique architecture and interior design in each location, the hotels were conceived by Balazs for young business travelers, whose cultural sophistication, typically far exceeds the scope of their wallets. The Standard is an inversion of the international corporate hotel model of the 1950s, which used sameness to reassure rather than variety to surprise or entertain. Flexible enough to accommodate renovations and new architecture, the only constants of the Standard brand are stylish attitude and attention to detail.

Balazs and his collaborators have created an inexpensive hotel that taps into the current infatuation with mid-twentieth-century modernism. The first Standard is located on the famed Sunset Strip in a building designed in 1964 as a motel. Film production designer Shawn Hausman combines classically modernist furnishings of the 1950s, 1960s, and 1970s—white shag carpet, Arco lamps, and plastic hanging bubble chairs—with contemporary pieces to create a "set" that evokes Rat Pack cool. The lobby is equipped with its own live art: in a vitrine behind the front desk a living diorama unfolds as actors and models take shifts reading and sleeping.

A proposed new building for the Standard branch in lower Manhattan was designed, in the words of principal Richard Gluckman, as "minimal capsules for living." These modular units generate a cellular structure that is visible behind the building's facade, a pattern of tinted and clear glass. In order to maximize interior space, his firm designed the rooms with only two primary architectural elements: a tinted translucent box for washing and dressing, and a wall-to-wall platform bed integral to the window wall. Only a flat-screen television belies the elegant austerity of the room.

The new Standard in downtown Los Angeles is housed in a marble and stainless steel International Style palazzo, built in 1956 as the headquarters of Superior Oil. Located in the heart of L.A.'s historic business district, this Standard, renovated by the local architecture firm Koning Eizenberg with interiors by Hausman, plays off the 1950s corporate aesthetic and its "techno-lust," simultaneously celebrating and spoofing them. The lobby's centerpiece is a furniture landscape designed by Vladimir Kagan, best known for his Boomerang sofas. Originally conceived by Kagan in the early 1970s, the lobby system is a series of interlocking sofas and tables on multiple levels. It is ideal for lounging and perching—as well as that time-honored L.A. tradition, seeing and being seen. —E.J.

The lobby of the Standard, Hollywood celebrates 1970s chic with Arco lamps and shag carpets.

TOP

Two views of the Standard, Hollywood.

MIDDLE

The Standard, Downtown L.A. is housed in a 1956 International Style office building. The guestrooms, seen in this full-scale model, are outfitted with sleek built-in furniture.

BOTTOM

Designer Vladimir Kagan's sketch shows his multilevel furniture landscape for the lobby of the Standard, Downtown L.A. The design was inspired by Kagan's own early 1970s Omnibus furniture system.

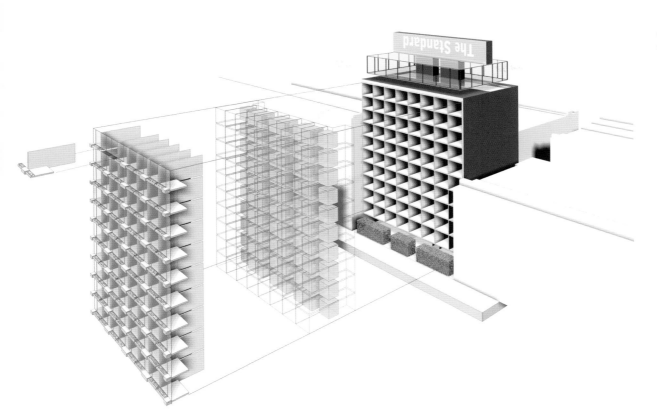

Design of the guestrooms in the proposed Standard, New York use a conventional module (bottom), which Gluckman Mayner Architects express on the building's exterior (top).

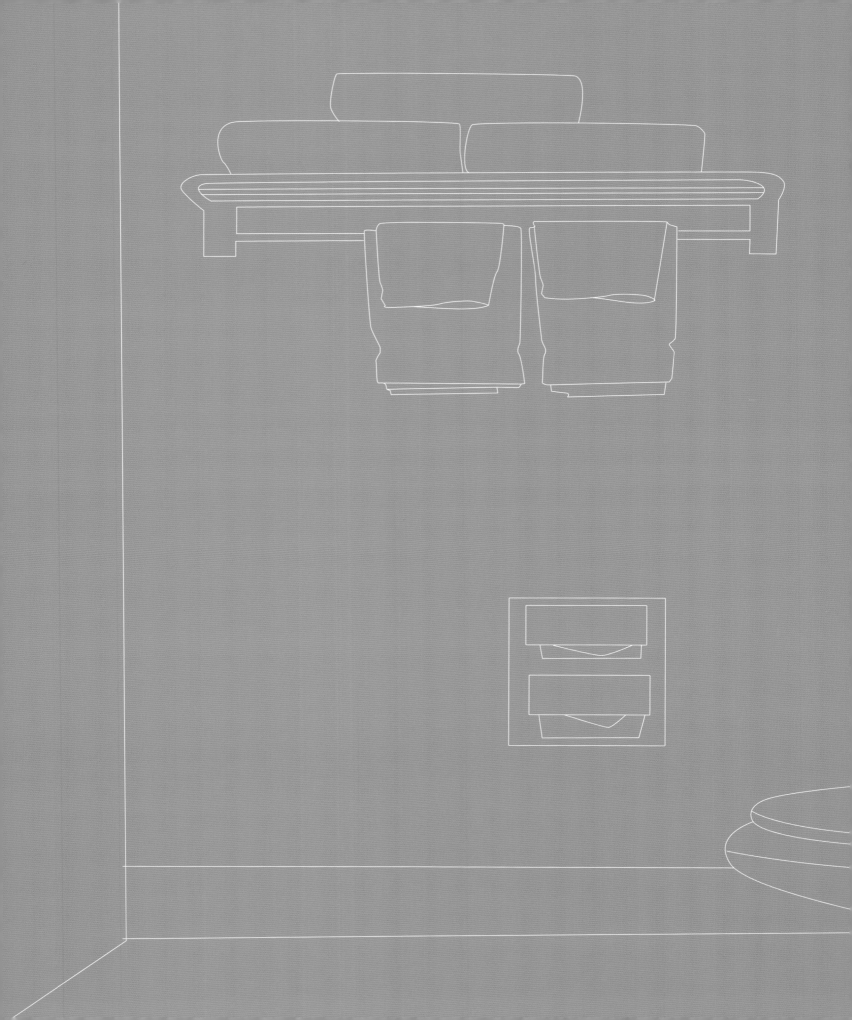

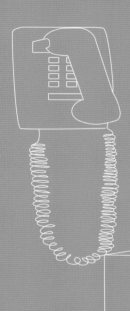

NATURAL HOTELS

NEW HOTEL FOR MAINSTREAM ECO-TOURISM

FTL

Since its emergence in the mid-1970s eco-tourism has grown from a miniscule segment of worldwide tourism to an estimated 20 to 30% today. This growth represents not just a change in number, but a change in kind: new eco-tourists are less purist than their predecessors, who truly "roughed it" without creature comforts, and demand lodging with some of the amenities of a mainstream hotel.

Geared toward "entry-level eco-tourists," as designer Todd Dalland calls them, his proposed New Hotel for Mainstream Eco-Tourism offers its guests a combination of "remote and pristine nature, environmental awareness, soft adventure, personal fitness, and a high level of luxury and attention." Dalland is a principal of FTL, the New York design and engineering firm well known for such structures as New York's 7th on Sixth fashion tents, the concert pavilion at Baltimore's Inner Harbor, and the retractable entry room for NASA's new space shuttle.

Planned for a beachfront in Costa Rica, the New Hotel for Mainstream Eco-Tourism combines an open-air Village Center with small clusters of guest cabanas dispersed for minimal environmental impact. The Village Center includes reception, dining facilities, shops, a spa, and a nonchlorinated swimming pond. The resort offers activities such as swimming, snorkeling, hiking, and kayaking, but not golf and tennis, which require razing or paving vast land areas and large quantities of water and pesticides. The Living Area comprises ten clusters of five guest pavilions each.

All the buildings are situated to take advantage of the sun's movement, of wind patterns, and of the climate. The design employs the most ecological mechanical systems: solar-powered heating for water, insulating glass windows, composting toilets, photovoltaic solar panels, freshwater cisterns, and a gray (nonpotable) water system for toilet flushing and irrigation. Structures and walkways on sensitive parts of the site are elevated on wood piles, set behind the sand dunes with views over them.

Dalland and his firm have investigated a variety of shapes for the roofs and materials for the walls. All are based on tensile fabric over a simple wood-frame structure. Fabric roofs are waterproof, ecologically sound due to their long lifespan, and, in the hands of FTL, visually striking. Tensile canopies protect visitors from the sun and rain. Fabrics, however, do not entirely block sound, so local plants have been placed between the guest pavilions for sound absorption. The ocean, the wildlife, and the wind provide natural ambient noise that also masks the sounds of other guests.

Like the natural hotels of the nineteenth century, the New Hotel for Mainstream Eco-Tourism unites tourists with nature in a sublime environment, but updates this concept to reflect today's environmental concerns. "The perception of being in the vanguard is important to eco-tourists," says Dalland. "They know they are participating in a capitalistic venture, but it is a capitalistic venture with vision and conscience."

—E.J.

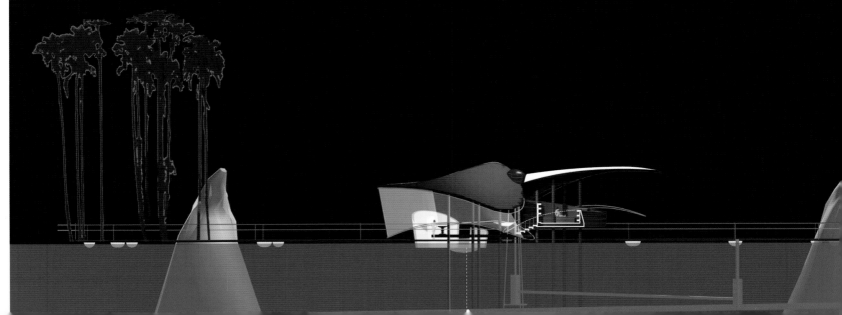

ROY

OKAVANGO DELTA SPA

OKAVANGO DELTA, BOTSWANA 1997

OUTSIDE VALDEZ, ALASKA 2001

WIND RIVER LODGE
CANCER ALLEY

BETWEEN BATON ROUGE AND NEW ORLEANS, LOUISIANA 2000

Under the direction of South African–born architect Lindy Roy, New York–based ROY has recently designed three resorts that are contemporary interpretations of the sublime: nature is experienced intensely as both dangerous and pleasurable, awesome yet safe. In an ever-changing spectacle, deserts convert to swamps, and icy wastelands transform before visitors' eyes into lush fields. Even the grotesque display of nature polluted by industrialization can be enjoyed through visiting toxic sites.

OKAVANGO DELTA SPA

Sited deep within the delta of Botswana's Okavango River, the Okavango Delta Spa (now a project on hold) was commissioned by Uncharted Africa as an extreme wildlife experience. At its annual peak in the winter, when floodwaters rush southward from Angola, the delta's low level of water covers some 15,000 sq. km (5800 sq. mi) of the Kalahari Desert. As the floodwaters recede, fresh grazing land is produced, drawing a stunning parade of migratory herds of elephants, zebras, and wildebeests. At the

center of this constantly shifting landscape lies a perennial swamp where the proposed spa would be located.

The only way to reach this remote resort is via plane or helicopter. ROY's design comprises fixed, tethered, and free-floating elements. Thatch-roofed guest pavilions, including a bar, dining-room, and seven sleeping pods, are set within natural clearings in the swamp's beds of papyrus. High-tech tent fabric and mosquito netting can be drawn along the edge of the thatch roofs, which are oriented to maximize shade and take advantage of shifting winds. A floating fiberglass spa is moored to each sleeping pod. Buoyant wood and fiberglass tracks weave through the swamp to connect the pods to natural "islands" created over many centuries, but now abandoned, by termites. In addition there are four floating "meditation pavilions" and a small swimming pool that can be maneuvered via outboard motor or docked in the shade of the bar. The steel-mesh pool offers vacationers the thrill of swimming safely amid the delta's population of crocodiles.

Okavango Delta Spa offers a secluded wildlife experience on a series of "islands" for sleeping, dining, and swimming.

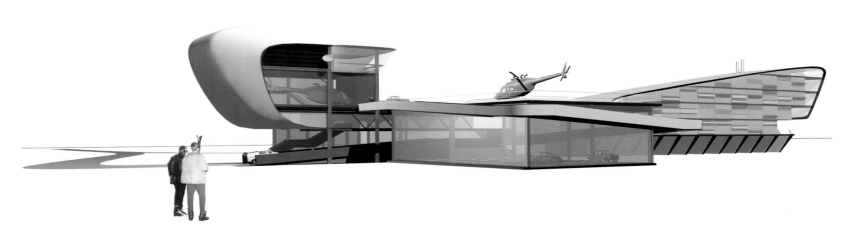

Reachable only by helicopter, the Wind River Lodge is an extreme ski resort, whose bold shape and color will announce its presence in the snow-clad landscape.

WIND RIVER LODGE

The Wind River Lodge, commissioned by a company of the same name and under construction soon, is a twenty-six-room facility organized around the activities of "extreme skiing." In this part of southern Alaska, brave sports lovers enjoy breathtaking glacial ridges and peaks up to 2.7 km (8800 ft) high. The site is blanketed by as much as 3 m (10 ft) of snow, and the body of the hotel is raised on concrete fins to clear this maximum snow line.

A colorful, iconic helipad announces the resort's presence in the all-white landscape. Visitors arrive via helicopter, like James Bond, and follow paramilitary procedures, from attending briefings and checking gear to participating in avalanche survival training. In the evening skiers can relax after the day's strenuous activities. The hotel's large, snow-covered roof is the ideal backdrop for photographing the day's "returning heroes." Large windows in the lounge provide views of the helipad and the awesome landscape beyond. But skiing is not the only attraction. Melting snow in the springtime floods the area, and within weeks—owing to twenty hours of sunlight per day—voracious plant growth transforms the formerly frozen site into a lush field of wildflowers and navigable waterways.

Cancer Alley is a conceptual project on the Mississippi River between Baton Rouge and New Orleans. Within thirty-five years the area's chief industry, oil refinery, will probably be depleted, and ROY proposes replacing the traditional economic base with tourism by using river barges for a motel (left), drive-in movie theater (center), and swimming pool.

CANCER ALLEY

ROY's Cancer Alley, a critical conceptual project, is located in the 160 km (100 m) stretch of the Mississippi River between Baton Rouge and New Orleans, where more than 150 industrial plants produce 25% of the nation's petrochemicals. Photographer Richard Misrach's images of the area inspired the project. The area reports the most concentrated toxic emissions in the air, land, and water within the United States, and the residents—predominantly poor African Americans—suffer from high rates of cancer and asthma. By 2035 the area's natural gas and oil reserves will probably be depleted and the industrial companies will leave. ROY's project proposes what could be dubbed "toxic tourism" as part of the area's post-industrial economic base. In addition to industry, the area features historic antebellum plantations and a rich cultural tradition of music and cuisine.

The Cancer Alley design uses the Mississippi's ubiquitous industrial barges, either singly or in groups, as floating modular landscapes. Barge-based libraries, sport facilities, and playgrounds would serve local communities. Because shoreline soil is largely contaminated, barges could also be planted with vegetable gardens. ROY has also designed new motels, parking lots, jazz cafés, casinos, and drive-in movie theaters on barges for tourists, who would arrive via New Orleans. Rarely has pollution been rendered so glamorous.

—D.A.

Dre Wapenaar

TREE TENT
1998

2001 # ARTCAMP

The original hotel—the tent—dates to ancient times, but today Dutch sculptor Dre Wapenaar creates tents that are more than places in which to sleep. He designs them as communication arenas: venues for spontaneous meetings. "The tent is a language well known all over the world," says Wapenaar. Wapenaar's brightly colored canvas and steel designs are based on the circle, which, he says, "is an ancient idea about being in a group, being protected, and being embraced." These qualities elicit the ideal emotional state for the interactions he likes to provoke.

Wapenaar's tents are "functional art"—formally beautiful sculptures for real situations or events. BBQ Tent has a fireplace and is sized for a party. Shower Tent can be used on beaches or in forests. Newspaper Kiosk is a conical tent filled with books and newspapers and a circular bench that seats six. Future projects include tents in which to give birth and to grieve. Until 1998 Wapenaar and a small team of assistants made the tents by themselves. Today he designs and builds a prototype of each tent himself, and then a factory produces them. Still, they are expensive, unique objects.

Two of Wapenaar's recent projects serve as overnight lodging. Tree Tent is a green sleeping pod originally designed for eco-protestors that hangs from a tree (see page 24). Three have recently been installed at a campground in the Netherlands, where they sleep four people each and cost $25 per night—a bargain considering the purchase price of $20,000. Wapenaar has started to design mini-villages rather than individual tents. A group of campground owners commissioned him in 2001 to create Artcamp, a cluster of five colorful tents in nature. One of them, Lovers' Tent, is made especially for couples. Raised above the others for privacy, it features a romantic skylight for star-gazing. Artcamp tents, which can be rented for $60 per night, are now being duplicated at three more Dutch campsites.

Eating, drinking, sleeping, and making love—although all of these activities take place in Wapenaar's tents, their creator considers them "still a sculpture, a live sculpture."

—E.J.

Artcamp is a cluster of brightly colored tents that can be rented at a campsite in Garderen, the Netherlands.

Architecture Research Office

NEW YORK NATURE HOTEL

NEW YORK CITY 2002

One of the most distinctive features of city parks is the contrast between their rolling, picturesque landscapes and the vertical, hard-edged structures that surround them. Although all urban parks share this dichotomy, parks in New York City—especially Central Park—are arguably the most extreme examples. Designed by Architecture Research Office (ARO) for this book and exhibition, the New York Nature Hotel bridges this urban divide. A prototypical seasonal resort to be erected in the city's parks, the Nature Hotel was initially proposed for construction in the summer of 2002 in the Arthur Ross Terrace and Garden at Cooper-Hewitt, National Design Museum. Using the vocabulary of Manhattan's gridiron street plan, the Nature Hotel is a tower made of scaffolding—itself an urban element—with walls draped in the mesh fabric that temporarily sheathes construction sites. ARO's hotel is a vertical campsite—a mini-skyscraper set among the trees.

Within the open structure, guests sleep next to birds and branches. The top floor is a unique deck for observing the city skyline within a frame of surrounding treetops. The scaffolding's minimal and temporary footprint allows the Nature Hotel to be put up in any park without leaving detrimental effects. This aspect, combined with the modular nature of scaffolding, means that the hotel can be built to service events— concerts, movies, and other performances—during the peak tourism months of summer. Guests in ARO's urban/natural hybrid sleep in the great outdoors while gaining exclusive night-time access to parks, "roughing it" in the big city. —D.A.

Constructed of scaffolding and clad in camouflage fabric, the New York Nature Hotel is digitally rendered here within Central Park. The hotel is a new kind of treehouse in which metal branches support hammock beds.

Rockwell Group

ART'OTEL

The Rockwell Group's Art'otel in London brings the natural hotel to the city: it is adjacent to the Tate Britain museum and overlooks the River Thames. The Red Sea Group, owner of the Berlin Art Hotels, hired Rockwell Group to design the Riverbank's public spaces and its specialty guestrooms. Rockwell's challenge was to create a "must-see" design that would attract people to an area not known for hotels and entertainment. Using a vocabulary of organic materials and nearly imperceptible transitions between interior and exterior, the Art'otel is a spectacular, theatrical urban garden. As in all of Rockwell Group's work, this motif permeates every aspect of the design.

The guest's experience begins in the driveway. Visitors arrive under a porte-cochère fashioned like an outdoor living-room, complete with a burning fireplace, oversized chaises and ottomans made of hedges and birch, and a plush carpet of grass and stone. The natural metaphor continues with a pair of unusual automatic doors into the atrium lobby: a floating, woodsy curtain of twigs and leaves sandwiched between panes of glass. The multistory atrium lobby—today a mainstay of the international corporate hotel—has been transformed here into a 12 m (39 ft) high arbor in bamboo, moss, and cast glass. The architects have even included a covered and heated exterior lounge contiguous with the lobby that can be used all year round. To make such a place appealing in a city not known for its inviting climate, Rockwell Group included an enormous glass fireplace and lots of small groupings of comfortable furniture.

Each of the Rockwell-designed guestrooms is styled like a private garden bedroom. A wall that automatically glows when the guest inserts the keycard in the door provides a warm welcome, carrying the public atrium motif through to the private guestroom. Even the bathroom is a landscaped stage, viewable through its glass walls and only partially veiled with twigs.

The Art'otel has all the architectural elements of the modern urban hotel—the porte-cochère, atrium lobby, and lounges and bars—dressed in natural garb. The American Rockwell Group combines the urban and natural hotel types by building on the English landscape tradition, particularly the picturesque. Their Art'otel is naturalistic—refined, luxurious, and knowingly artificial.

—E.J.

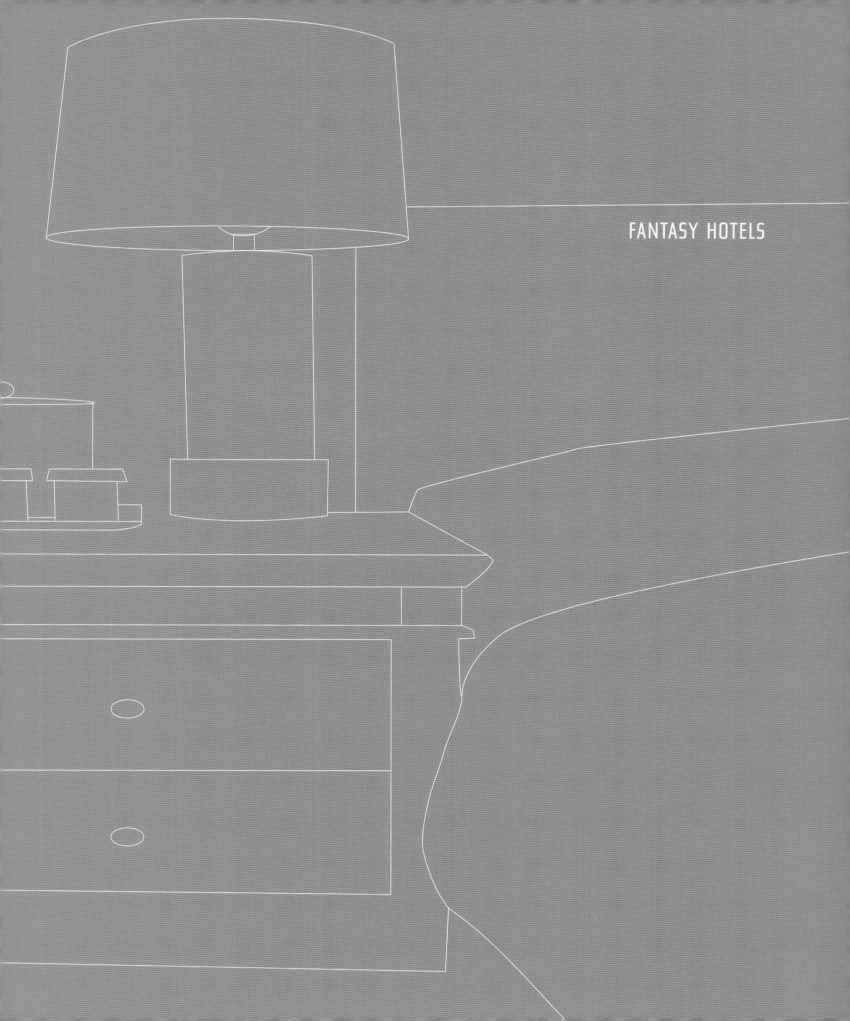

FANTASY HOTELS

BURJ AL-ARAB

W. S. Atkins

Located on a specially built island off the shore of Dubai, the Burj al-Arab (Arabian Tower) is reached only via private helicopter or via causeway traversed only by the hotel's Rolls Royces. Thus begins a hotel experience defined by luxury, new technology, and exclusivity. Dubai's ruler, Sheikh Muhammed bin Rashid al Maktoum, commissioned the hotel as a new world landmark, just one of his efforts to transform the city into a globally important center of Middle Eastern culture and business. In this way the Burj al-Arab is the twenty-first-century embodiment of the tradition of building a grand urban hotel to advertise a city's new world-class status.

Like its predecessors the Burj al-Arab is a catalog of extremes. Designed by W. S. Atkins, a London-based multinational engineering and architecture firm, the structure is the tallest dedicated hotel (and the thirteenth tallest building) in the world. Billowing like a ship's sail, a reference to the importance of water transport in the Persian Gulf, a curving, Teflon-coated membrane that extends the full height of the building is the hotel's most dramatic feature. Highly sophisticated structural and mechanical systems heavily fortify the Burj al-Arab against the harsh desert climate, where temperatures reach 55 degrees Celsius (130 degrees Fahrenheit). During the day the membrane filters the intense sunlight; at night, it is a screen for a computerized light show.

The extraordinary exterior is complemented by an equally fantastic interior. A geyser, reaching heights of 30 m (100 ft), dominates the building's V-shaped atrium. Throughout, 22-karat gold leaf covers everything from columns to vases, totaling more than 2,000 sq. m (21,000 sq. ft). There are more than two hundred guestrooms, each a two-story suite with its own private butler—just one of many over-the-top amenities. Room rates range from $900 to astronomical heights: $7,000,000 buys 1001 fabulous nights in this Arabian fantasy.   —E.J.

The sail-shaped tower of the Burj al-Arab, the tallest hotel in the world, is located on a man-made island.

LEFT

An enormous cylindrical
aquarium and mirrored ceiling
shift perceptions in the hotel's
underground restaurant. In a
bleak desert setting, the Burj
al-Arab is conceived as a tourist
destination in its own right.

RIGHT

Lavishly appointed two-story
guest suites contain such
amenities as circular bed platforms, large-screen televisions,
and their own butler. Room
rates start at $900 per night.

FAR RIGHT

A circular geyser, which
reaches heights of 30 m
(100 ft), dominates the hotel's
fantastically decorated
atrium lobby.

ROOM 12

ROOM 24

ROOM 44

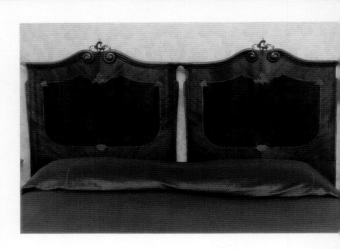

ROOM 47

Sophie Calle

"THE HOTEL"

1983

For just over three weeks in early 1981 French artist Sophie Calle worked as a chambermaid in a Venetian hotel she describes as Hotel C, where she was responsible for twelve guestrooms. In addition to cleaning each room, she opened drawers and suitcases and read the occupants' personal papers. Probably not the first maid to spy on hotel guests, Calle went one important step further: she meticulously arranged and photographed the guests' personal effects and created a work of art from them. "I observed through details," Calle recalled, "lives which remained unknown to me."

The Hotel is a series of diptychs: one image is a detail of the bed, the other a photographic grid of shoes, letters, underwear, and toiletries arranged like police evidence of a crime scene. An accompanying text, written by Calle, is a detailed stream-of-consciousness description. "A small bag on the luggage stand," reads the entry from "Room 30," which also observes, "A beautifully ironed silk nightgown lies on the chair that

has been pulled up by the bed: it clearly has never been worn." Calle learned from a passport in the room that the guest, M. L., was "male sex, Italian nationality, born in 1946 in Rome, his place of residence, five foot seven, blue eyes."

The Hotel is typical of Calle's work, which often deals with surveillance and usually records the forced intersections between her life and those of strangers. For example, she has followed people for days, photographing their activities. She once found a man's address book and called everyone in it to find out about the owner's life, and finally published her findings in a newspaper. In *The Hotel*, she transgresses the boundaries between public and private, fact and fiction. Such boundary-hopping is a unique feature of the hotel as a temporary home. Indeed, Calle describes her surveillance as "stealing by looking."

—D.A.

Four headboard images from The Hotel *show the range of decor at the hotel where artist Sophie Calle was briefly employed.*

R O O M   2 4

Monday March 2, 1981, 10:30a.m. I go into room 24, the pink one. The twin beds have been slept in. A strange feeling of "déjà vu" comes over me. Various images blend together. Days and clients all run together in my mind. Haven't I already visited these? The first things I notice are the books on the table: Alain Gerber's La Couleur Orange and a French Italian dictionary. In the closet: the usual clothes of an ordinary couple, photographic equipment in a camera case, an empty suitcase. The drawer is stuffed with handkerchiefs, medication for a deficient pancreas and Caporal Gauloises cigarettes.

I empty the handbag on the floor: sugar cubes, Tampax, pink lipstick, postal checks made out to Paulette B., old tickets for a Xenakis concert and an agenda. On the first page I read: "In the event of my death, everything I own will go to Mr. François G., exclusively". Signed Paulette B. in a childish, touching handwriting. Under the heading Notes, this figure: 23485,68, the address of a rest home in Versailles, a sentence: "Between the age of one year to eighteen months, the chamois is called an "éterlou", plus a quote from Malraux I find hard to decipher. What I think I read is: "C'est bien la première civilisation blanche mais c'est aussi la façon étincelante d'un monde meurt. Nous n'unissons pas sans peine à l'Iliade ni même à l'Odyssée ces cours ou ces premiers murs coiffés de plumes d'autruche, inclinant leurs lunes devant des Phèdres aux seins offerts au-dessous d'un chaud bouillonnement de trilles. A. Malraux, NRF, 1954, page 93."

On the agenda are the following notes: 30.1 Unemployment Bureau, 6.2 "l'heure du loup" (the wolf's hour), 10.2 Unemployment Bureau, text of verdict, 14.2 Unemployment Bureau, 20.2 Unemployment Bureau. Further on is a list of expenses, in particular for the trip to Venice: departure 200,000l., or 3,450F (28.2 gasoline 270, meal 45, highway toll 103.1.3: tunnel 56, cap Venice 100, taxi 90, meal 300). In the bag is also the reservation at the Hotel C. until March 6, a customer's certificate from a cleaner in Bordeaux, a blue paper in the name of Paulette B., born May 1, 1956: it is a "baccalauréat" diploma, "série moderne", dated July 1956. Nine voter registration cards, all out of date, for the years 1964 to 1980. A letter sent from Mexico to Paulette B. in 1972, which reads in French: "News at last from your American cousin. I'm beginning to get used to things. What is good about this country is building something new, from scratch... she goes on about the wild animals, local folklore, the creation of a cooperative)... What families would need when they get there is pigs, cows, goats, hens, bananas, oranges, lemons, grapefruits, pineapples...and we think that by 1976, the first farmers will be able to come over and work for themselves. Best regards, Albert." Then there is a postcard mailed the same year: "As you can see, we've opted for Italy this year for three weeks. It is stiflingly hot in Florence. We've done a thorough job of visiting this lovely city and we're now about to go and cool off in the Alps. Best regards, Monique V." Then a certain years ago...On the floor are two suitcases, one on top of the other. One of them is spilling over with clothes. I've had enough, I don't go through it. The other is locked. It belongs to a certain G., a seafaring captain who lives in

Versailles. It is heavy and full.

Tuesday 3. 10:20a.m. On the table is Gerber's book open on page 37. Beside it are two other books: the Blue-Guide-Italy and a bound book called Intimité de Venise. A red flannelette nightgown is hanging in the bathroom. Time is short. The suitcase is still locked. I don't want to linger.

Wednesday 4. 11a.m. Nothing seems to have changed in the room. Everything is in the same place. I head straight for the handbag. In it I find two passports. One is in the name of Paulette B, secretary, French nationality, five foot three, born May 1, 1956, green eyes, home address Bordeaux, and a single stamp for entry into Malaga in 1976. The other is in the name of François G., French nationality, born January 4, 1910, blue eyes, five foot seven, home address Versailles, same stamp for Malaga. Inside Paulette's passport are six passport photographs (she, I imagine from childhood to adulthood). In the bottom of the handbag I find a small key. It opens the suitcase, where I glimpse men's clothes and a book by Jean d'Ormesson Au Plaisir de Dieu. I close it very quickly. I am afraid. I put the key back in the handbag and straighten up the room.

Thursday 5. 11:30a.m. They have been to see "Idomeneo" at the Venice theater (I see the tickets in the wastebasket). The bed is full of crumbs, and a geometric sign on the bedsheets catches my eye. The little black scarf is still hanging in the closet. Tomorrow they'll be gone.

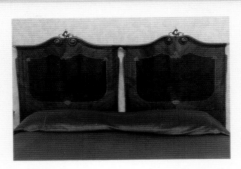

ROOM 47

Monday March 2, 1981. 10:00 a.m. My first sensation is of banality and an exemplary neatness. Nothing on the table, empty drawers, no clothing showing. A single book, the Guide Michelin Italie has been placed on the left-hand bedside table. On the floor, an attaché case. Inside it, a red hot-water bottle. In the bathroom, nothing in particular to catch one's eye: ordinary toiletries, some Microlax for constipation, some Calèche perfume, contraceptive pills. There's only the wardrobe left to explore, I open it. On the left, the man: Cacharel and Daniel Hechter shirts, gray suits, ties... On the right, the woman: corduroy trousers, wool skirts... The suitcase has a sticker on it: "M. et Mme C... Paris, 17." It contains three pairs of panties, bathmits, three pairs of socks, striped pajamas, a sachet of sandalwood, some coat hangers, a clothes brush, a hairdryer, an Olympus camera, a plastic bag with the dirty laundry (three pairs of panties, a bra, a blouse), some leather soap, a book called Belle Italie, an electric extension cord, some keys, a guide to French hotels, a list of the Sofitel chain of hotels, a pocket torch, some rugs and shoe polish, a wallet. In the wallet I find the following documents: two international driver's licenses in the names of Antoine C., born in 1943, and Emmanuelle C., born in 1948. Bills from some other Venetian hotels (they spent the night of February 26 in room 18 of the Hotel Cavaletto and the night of February 28 in room 10 of the Luna) and a diary in the name of Eliane C. I check out how she spends her time. February 1 at noon: tennis in Neuilly. February 5: bank lunch. February 6: flowers,

elephant, English dinner. February 10: Carita, 11:00 a.m. February 19: lunch. February 28: holidays. Nothing for January or March. In the "Notes" section of the book, a page is devoted to their water consumption: "Hot water: 6.6.79, bedrm.: 11m³, bathrm.: 14m³, 10.20.79, bedrm.: 16m3, bathrm.: 48m³; 2.10.80, bedrm.: 20m³, bathrm.: 70m³; 6.7.80, bedrm.: 24m²... On a second page, various dates: "Monsieur C: 11.12.1912; Madame C: 26.1 (the woman's year of birth is not mentioned). Laurent: 1.24.71; Johanna: 1.24.71," then a list of books: "Mémoires de l'Afghanistan, La route des Indes, Îles et presqu'îles de l'Extrême-Orient"... On a last page, the following list written in French: "Clouds and san (400 Asa 125e). Stakes with seagulls and Isola San Giorgio to the north. The base of the first column near the Ducal Palace. A guest framed by two windows of Florian's which reflect the square. Chandeliers under the colonnade and view towards the cathedral. Red and blue mooring posts. The Arsenal. Nun dressed in white going into the hospital. Two pigeons billing and cooing." The address book contains a dozen home telephone numbers as well as the following numbers: Hôtel Bristol, BHV, BMW, neighbor, Carita, CFDT, Cacharel, Antar, framer, Galeries Lafayette, Golfe, Lévitan, psychotherapist; Mrs. V., nurse; Miss D., jeweler, painter, concierge. Social Security, department store. Sucaflor, taxis, Harry's Bar, Blvd. Haussmann Printemps, Place d'Italie Printemps, Dessanges hair salon, the hospice... I postpone my reading to go and do room 43.

Tuesday 3. 10:00 a.m. The Guide Michelin has been put away in the wardrobe and replaced on the bedside table by a list of Banque Hervet cash machines. There's an umbrella lying around. On the left, the person sleeps with two pillows; on the right, with one. The brown raincoat is no longer in the wardrobe (it's raining) and a blue Cardin torch. I go back to the diary. In the calendar, the days 1.3., 1.4., 1.9, 1.17., 1.18, 1.23, 1.31, 2.1, 2.6, 2.8, 2.14, 2.15, 2.20, 2.28, 3.1, 3.2 have been crossed out in blue. The 2, 3, 4, and 5 are marked with a cross and February 6 and 8 are crossed out and marked with a cross.

Wednesday 4. 10:30 a.m. The Guide Michelin has been brought back out and, along with the list of Sofitel hotels, has been put on the right-hand table. A flat packet lies on the bed. I open it: it is a poster of the Venice Carnival.

Thursday 5. 11:15 a.m. I go into room 47. A second umbrella has been set beside the first. They have brought a spray can of Pronto, a cleaning product.

Friday 6. 10:30 a.m. They have gone. On the bed they have left a tube of pink lipstick. There are towels lying around the bathroom.

"LOVE HOTELS, JAPAN"

Photographs by Peter Marlow

In Japan, where homes are small, walls are thin, and many generations live together, "love hotels" sell privacy for sex. From their beginnings in the 1950s as an alternative to more expensive traditional inns, they have grown into a multibillion-dollar industry, available in every price range. Rooms can be rented overnight (dubbed "sleep/stay") or for just a few hours ("rest").

Peter Marlow's series of photographs of typical love hotels in Kyoto convey the guests' experiences. Love hotels are built around the Japanese preoccupation with discretion that honors the deep divide between public and private behavior. Throughout their entire stay guests never see hotel staff and rarely other guests. Driveways are hidden, and clip-on blocks obscure guests' license plates. Rooms are chosen at the front desk from a backlit menu of pictures of interiors. Once a room has been rented, the light behind its picture is turned off. Money and room keys are exchanged through a narrow slot. The elevator takes guests up to their floor only; stopping on other floors is impossible. The hotels' high standards of cleanliness reinforce their respectability.

The decor, however, reflects the national taste for kitsch. Rooms are themed, and a single hotel might offer a variety of choices, from a tropical setting to *Gone with the Wind* to S & M. Among the more common is a cartoonish romanticism typical of Western hotels in Las Vegas and Niagara Falls. Rooms are equipped with robes and slippers, karaoke machines, mini-bars stocked with sexual aids and alcohol, video cameras, and television showing pornography. Marlow's photographs reveal that within a culture of propriety, society provides discreet outlets for hedonism.

—E.J.

Payment and room keys are exchanged discreetly via a blind pass-through at the registration desk.

FAR LEFT

At the Hotel Dance, photos of available rooms allow customers to choose the theme or decor they prefer. When a room is rented, its image is darkened on the menu board.

NEAR LEFT

Room service at the Hotel Tiffany is served through a double-doored compartment in the wall so that staff never see the guests.

NEAR RIGHT

The childlike Western-style romantic decor of this room at the Hotel Dance offers guests a simple fantasy.

FAR RIGHT

Sex toys are sold from a mini-bar in this room at the Hotel la Forêt. Microphones for karaoke are seen at right.

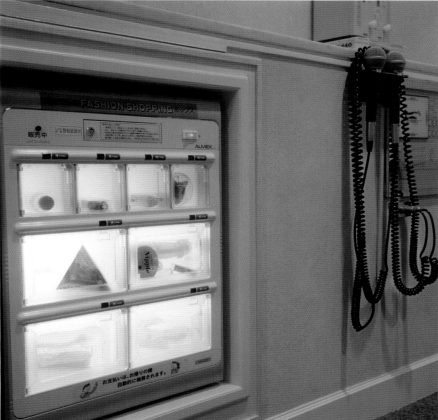

Tom Sachs

"COMPACT FULL FEATURE HOTEL ROOM"

2002

Inspired by commercialism and technology, and operating as a sculptor, engineer, bricoleur, do-it-yourselfer, and cultural critic, Tom Sachs creates full-scale models of real objects and environments. Sachs has designed and built a guillotine plastered with Chanel logos, a Prada plunger, and Hermès hand grenades. A 1999 exhibition of Sachs's work at the Manhattan gallery of Mary Boone resulted in her arrest for giving away live ammunition in the artist's Hermès-style air-sickness bags.

In addition to designer brands, Sachs is also drawn to hotel culture. His *Compact Full Feature Hotel Room* was conceived for installation in *New Hotels for Global Nomads*, although it grew out of an idea originally developed by Sachs and *Nest* magazine founder, art director, and editor-in-chief Joseph Holtzman. Fitted within the 17 sq. m (180 sq. ft) master dressing-room of the Andrew Carnegie mansion, the museum's historic home, the work is largely impractical depiction of a functional room—complete with bed, toilet, sink, shower, surveillance system, television, and phone. Like *Lil T's Toilet Town*, Sachs's complex, operable recreation of a bathroom, the *Compact Room* is made of everyday materials, in this case bubblewrap, plywood, foamcore, and duct tape. Sachs is part of a larger art movement interested in bricolage. Other artists in this group, whose work Sachs dubs "hobby crafts," include Tim Hawkinson, Richard Wentworth, Panamarenko, and Toland Grinnell. In Sachs's work, amateurish disregard for fine finishes

mocks modern American culture's obsession with perfect appearance. He calls his art "props" for those who "repair instead of replace."

More typically American is Sachs's fondness for consumer objects. The *Compact Room* is furnished with a full-scale, mocked-up Eames lounge chair and ottoman (with prominent Herman Miller logos), and an Eero Saarinen coffee table. In his design sketch for the project—itself a bricolage of scotch tape, paper, and manila file folder—Sachs lists the room's contents in detail: robes, showercap, condoms, Band-aids, aspirin, and so on. Design references connect the project to a constellation of movies (*Patton*), art (Oldenburg), and design (Zanuso and Colombo).

Earlier works by Sachs examined the hotel as inspiration for art. In 1997 he took part in the Gramercy International Art Fair at the Chateau Marmont in Los Angeles. In his makeshift studio in the hotel pornographic film stars created their own sculptures, using glue guns, trash, and duct tape. His 1998 *Sony Outsider* is a kind of Japanese capsule hotel built within a full-scale mock-up of the Fat Man atomic bomb dropped on Nagasaki in 1945. Sachs's *Compact Full Feature Hotel Room* is a visual oxymoron within the highly ornate Carnegie mansion. Wedged into the smallest room in the house, Sachs's work encapsulates the hotel experience in an obsessively rendered fantasy.

—D.A.

Sachs's 1998 Sony Outsider *is a kind of Japanese capsule hotel encased in a full-scale mock-up of the Fat Man atomic bomb that was dropped on Nagasaki in 1945.*

Lil T's Toilet Town *(2000) is
Sachs's complex but operable
bathroom built of rough, industrial materials.*

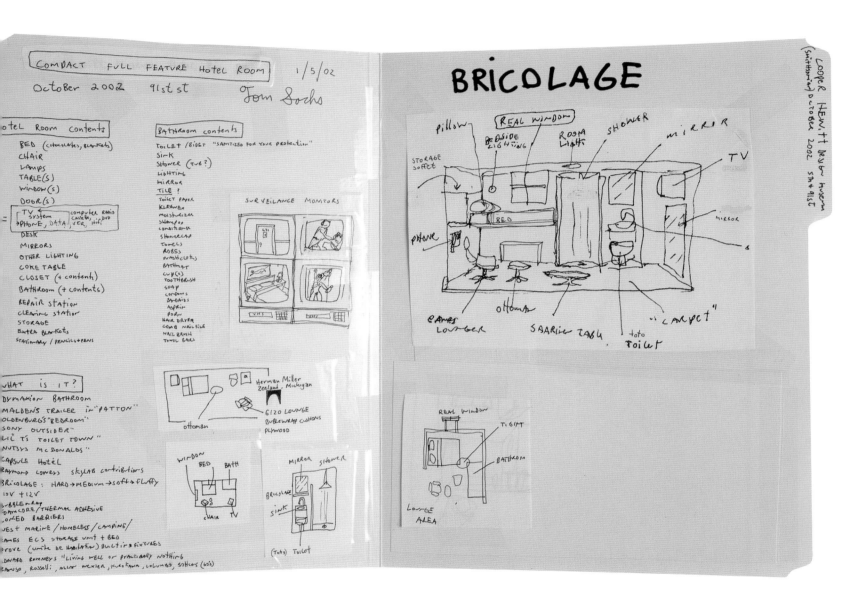

The artist's design sketch for the Compact Full Feature Hotel Room, *a bricolage environment specially created for* New Hotels for Global Nomads.

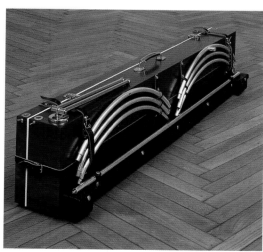

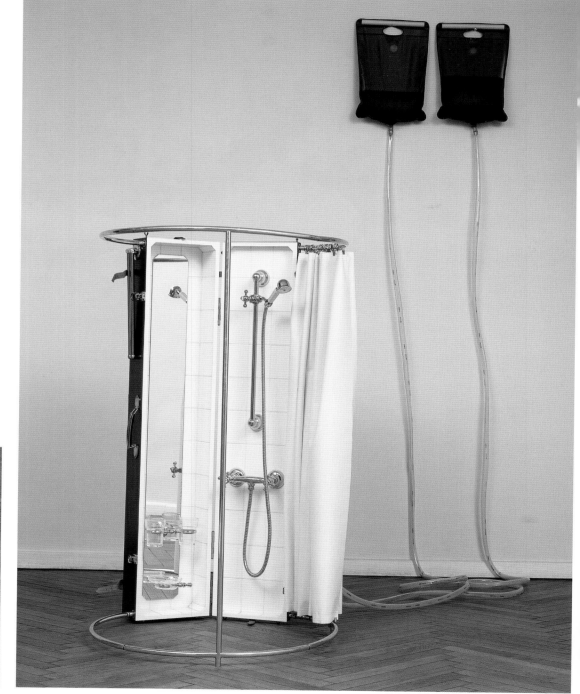

M. K. Kähne

"SANITARY FURNITURE"

1996–98

German artist M. K. Kähne creates portable devices—from surveillance systems to mini-bars—that aid the modern global traveler. Kähne focuses on men and aims to enhance their corporate lives with the stylishness of James Bond. *Sanitary Furniture* (Sanitärmobiliar) is a series of rich trunks of wood, leather, and stainless steel that open to reveal gleaming bathing facilities. One houses a shower; another, a bathtub; and others, full bathrooms equipped with toilets, urinals, sinks, and showers.

Kähne is an engineer-cum-craftsman. The operation manuals he writes for each of the pieces of *Sanitary Furniture* include technical specifications and drawings. He taught himself carpentry, plumbing, welding, and upholstery to achieve his highly finished work. His elaborate attention to craft and exquisite materials—including mahogany, porcelain, and chrome—fetishize the simple purpose for which his objects are made.

Kähne's usable art has been described by art critic Sabine Russ as "extravagant pragmatism" in which "the esthetically sublime is contrasted by the practically profane." In elevating the everyday *Sanitary Furniture* revives a cult of bodily hygiene and health from the 1920s and 1930s, when such architects as Le Corbusier, Ludwig Mies van der Rohe, and Richard Neutra created modernist bathrooms as sleek, high-art altars.

Part of the intricacy of Kähne's art pieces is the way each unit collapses into a beautiful, and seemingly transportable, piece of luggage. Kähne's sketches show how he intends his sanitary furnishings to be used by businessmen in suburban parks and office conference rooms, where they need never leave a meeting. But *Sanitary Furniture* could just as easily equip a hotel room, where standards of hygiene and style might not meet the expectations of the artist's mythic modern man.   —E.J.

This piece from the Sanitary Furniture *series is a fully functioning porcelain shower that opens up from a suitcase made of mahogany and chrome.*

Toland Grinnell

"PRIVATE DANCER"

2002

Artist Toland Grinnell's *Private Dancer* is a "fetish palace" that allows the well-heeled international nightclubber to travel with his or her own private performance space for erotic dancing in hotel rooms. Presented for the first time in *New Hotels for Global Nomads*, this elaborate pleasuredome folds in on itself to form a sleek, mobile trunk that hides its seductive secrets as its owner wheels it from city to city, room to room. "The hotel," says Grinnell, "is the most important fantasy space in our culture today."

Outfitted like a luxury sedan, with a black exterior and a tan interior complete with nickel-plated hardware, *Private Dancer* is three pieces of furniture in one: an upholstered chaise with Empire-style bolster pillow; a personal desk and vanity with folding chair; and a one-person shiny black dance floor with its own footlights and full-length mirror. Within a series of cabinets and drawers hides a surreal collection of accessories, from wigs and playing cards to dinner plates and silverware. Taken together, it forms an assembly line for a night of pleasure with twists—from makeup and preparation to performance and ritual to, finally, sex.

Grinnell, who believes that "the most fabulous objects made in almost every culture throughout time—from Polynesian statues to depictions of Christian saints to Picasso's drawings—have had a really high degree of perversity built into them," has since the late 1990s constructed intricate fantasy worlds that unfold from luxurious trunks and boxes. Each of his works, which he designs and handcrafts himself, is emblazoned with his trademarked "TG" logo, aligning the work with the world's most opulent brands, including Louis Vuitton. In fact, as early as the 1870s Vuitton created beds—and later, desks—that opened out from trunks for colonial explorers and celebrities. Grinnell blends a fascination for French style with an American appreciation for gadgetry. His *Machine for Living* of 2000 opens accordion-like to reveal a "survival kit" for a Rothschild, complete with a miniature piano, leather-bound library, champagne, bottled water, a safe deposit box with jewelry, and even an 18-karat gold exercise wheel for a pampered hamster.

In an age of high speed, endless travel, and chain hotels, the discerning nomad demands the same standards on the road that he or she enjoys in every aspect of his or her logo-clad life. Toland Grinnell's work offers old-world craftsmanship for modern desires. Don't leave home without it.

—E.J.

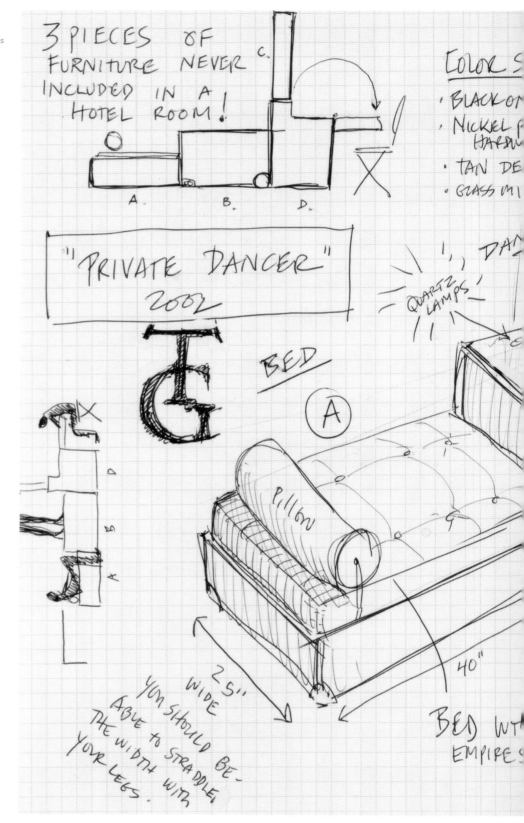

Grinnell's design sketch for Private Dancer, *a new work making its debut in* New Hotels for Global Nomads, *reveals an obsession with detail and a pragmatic understanding of mechanics for portability.*

3 PIECES OF FURNITURE NEVER INCLUDED IN A HOTEL ROOM!

A.   B.   D.

COLOR S
· BLACK O
· NICKEL
  HARD
· TAN DE
· GLASS M

"PRIVATE DANCER"
2002

TG

DA
QUARTZ LAMPS

BED

Ⓐ

Pillow

25"
WIDE

YOU SHOULD BE-
ABLE to STRADDLE
THE WIDTH WITH
YOUR LEGS.

40"

BED WT
EMPIRES

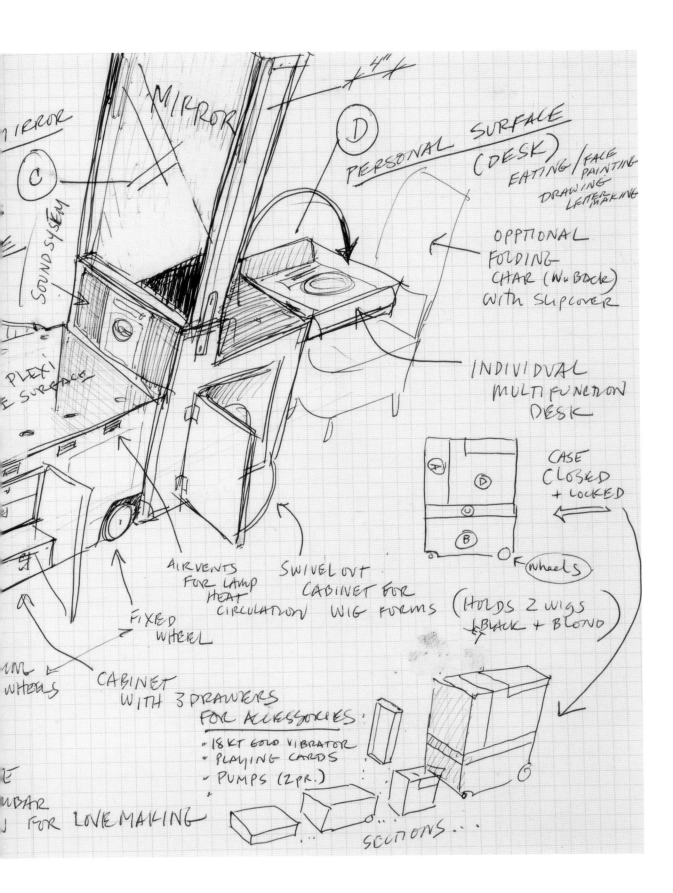

MIRROR

MIRROR

C

D PERSONAL SURFACE (DESK)
EATING/FACE PAINTING
DRAWING
LETTER MAKING

SOUND SYSTEM

OPPTIONAL FOLDING CHAIR (W. BACK) WITH SLIPCOVER

PLEXI E SURFACE

INDIVIDUAL MULTI FUNCTION DESK

CASE CLOSED + LOCKED

A
D
U
B
F Wheels

AIR VENTS FOR LAMP HEAT CIRCULATION

SWIVEL OUT CABINET FOR WIG FORMS (HOLDS 2 WIGS BLACK + BLOND)

FIXED WHEEL

NG WHEELS

CABINET WITH 3 DRAWERS FOR ACCESSORIES:
- 18 KT GOLD VIBRATOR
- PLAYING CARDS
- PUMPS (2 PR.)

BAR FOR LOVE MAKING

SECTIONS...

Maureen Connor

"ROLES PEOPLE PLAY"

2002

The word "construction" carries many meanings in the art of Maureen Connor. A recent group of wickedly funny and visually elegant installations combines films, furnishings, and photographs to explore the relationship between architecturally constructed space and socially constructed behavior. Key to appreciating Connor's work is the ability to enjoy the discomfort caused by her juxtapositions of ideal and real images. Connor's three-dimensional dissections of personal (often romantic) interaction include *Dancing Lessons* (1995), in which a staged scene of this awkward social ritual is intercut with Hollywood musicals. More recently, Connor's *Love (at first) Site* (1997–98) scrutinizes a trio of twentieth-century spaces with distinctive sexual pedigrees: an urban balcony as seen in Depression-era romantic films, a 1950s bachelor pad, and a late-1990s bedroom, complete with an interactive "morning after" game that lets visitors determine whether the just-ended one-night stand has any future.

Roles People Play, specially commissioned for *New Hotels for Global Nomads*, explores popular film depictions of hotels, as both physical setting and psychological context for a broad range of dramatic action. Furniture, videos, and simulated architectural space convey the social interactions that hotels foster. *Roles People Play* focuses on the door and the bed—the hotel sites that most compellingly suggest transition and transformation, fantasy and desire. In the installation viewers see a wall on which images of movie stars knocking on hotel-room doors are shown, on a split screen, with actors answering them. These simultaneous clips elicit the feelings of anticipation and suspense that typically occur at this highly charged boundary between public and private. Beyond the wall, an overscaled bed is outfitted with a complex arrangement of mirrors and video monitors showing beds in various guises, from perfectly made to voluptuously rumpled, that seem to shrink or expand. Through this illusion of spatial distortion, *Roles People Play* suggests that the hotel room and its centerpiece, the bed, go beyond the merely physical to become earthly altars to faith in sexual satisfaction.

—D.A.

Bachelor Pad, *which combined 1950s furniture with projections and audio, was one of three installations that made up Connor's* Love (at first) Site *(1997–98). Connor uses a similar aesthetic in* Roles People Play, *specially commissioned for* New Hotels for Global Nomads.

Ateliers Jean Nouvel

THE HOTEL

LUCERNE, SWITZERLAND 2000

Created by hotelier Urs Karli to compete with the grand Swiss hotels that frame outward views to mountains and lakes, this intimate hotel looks inward to the subconscious. "Film," Paris-based architect Jean Nouvel has said, describing his sources, "is our version of the Greek myths." In his design for The Hotel, Nouvel explores the edges between the hotel as a real architectural space and as a dream space fashioned by cinema. Each of the seven-story hotel's twenty-five guestrooms features an enlarged film still mounted on its ceiling and lit by sleek wall sconces reminiscent of footlights. From the work of his modern mythmakers—Almodóvar, Bertolucci, Fassbinder, Fellini, Buñuel, Lynch, and Greenaway—Nouvel has chosen to reproduce scenes with a strong sexual charge, cropped and angled for maximum theatrical effect. He has provided the hotel's guests with an intensified image of the reflections they would hope to see if they were in a honeymoon suite with a mirrored ceiling. Nouvel and artist Alain Bony painted the dark walls of the guestrooms to suggest vague, distorted reflections of the film still on the ceiling, creating a kind of surreal "after-image" not unlike our memories of favorite movie scenes. The minimalist styling of the furniture, custom-designed by Nouvel in matte stainless steel and Brazilian cherrywood, keeps the guests' focus on the drama overhead.

The hotel's ground-floor bar and seventy-seat restaurant continue the theme of a perceptual sleight of hand. Nouvel mixes mirrors, movie stills, and windows to alternately hide and reveal public spaces, like a sexy striptease. Canted mirrors behind the ground-floor windows reflect scenes both up and down; diners in the lower-level restaurant see street activity, while passersby glimpse the spectacle within.

Immersed in a cinematic world, the guests become actors in a larger film metaphor. From a distance the hotel's windows become mini-movie screens, turning local people into voyeurs. It's Alfred Hitchcock's *Rear Window* turned into architecture.   —D.A.

Movie stills depicting scenes of tension and sex are reproduced larger than life on the guestroom ceilings.

BIBLIOGRAPHY

Compiled by Randi Mates

Akin, David. "Aiming for the Moon." *Toronto Globe and Mail* (Oct. 20, 2001): F7.

Baimbridge, Richard. "Charting New Territory in Cyberspace: With the Help of a Modem, Fakeshop Brings Its Art to a Worldwide Audience." *Brooklyn Bridge* (March 1999): 32.

Barros, Rita, ed. *Chelsea Hotel: Fifteen Years*. New York: Camara Municipal de Lisboa, 1999.

Belle, John, and Maxinne Leighton. *Grand Central: Gateway to a Million Lives*. New York and London: W. W. Norton, 2000.

Berens, Carol. *Hotel Bars and Lobbies*. New York: McGraw-Hill, 1997.

"Best Hotel: Rockwell Group. W New York, New York City." *Interiors* (Jan. 2000): 40–43.

Blodgett, Peter. "Visiting the Realms of Wonder: Yosemite and the Business of Tourism, 1855–1916." *California History* 69, 2 (1990): 118–33.

Brucken, Carolyn E. "Consuming Luxury: Hotels and the Rise of Middle-Class Public Space, 1825–1860." Ph.D. diss., George Washington University, 1997.

Busch, Akiko. "Paradise Sustained." *Interiors* (June 2000): 78–81.

Caplan, Ralph, et al. *Bon Voyage: Designs for Travel*. New York: Cooper-Hewitt Museum, 1986.

Casciani, Stefano. "Paradise Hotel." *Domus* (November 2000): 64–71.

Corbett, Theodore. *The Making of American Resorts: Saratoga Springs, Ballston Spa, Lake George*. New Brunswick, N.J.: Rutgers University Press, 2001.

Cronstrom, Kendell. "The Standard Bearer." *Elle Decor* (Aug.–Sept. 1999): 202–205.

Croutier, Aleo Lytle. *Taking the Waters: Spirit, Art, Sensuality*. New York: Abbeville Press, 1992.

De Graaf, Jan. "Tourism, Mobility, and Architecture." *Archis* (1998–99): 70–79.

Denby, Elaine. *Grand Hotels: Reality and Illusion*. London: Reaktion Books, 1998.

Donzel, Catherine, et al. *Grand American Hotels*. New York: Vendome, 1989.

Dunlap, David W. "From Front Office to Front Desk: Landmark Office Buildings Being Turned into Hotels." *New York Times*, Sept. 10, 2000, sec. 11.

———. "'Most Hated Hotel' Reclaims Its Floridian Flamboyance." *New York Times*, Nov. 8, 2000, D8.

End, Henry. *Interiors' Second Book of Hotels*. New York: Whitney Library of Design, 1978.

Finney, Garrett, and Victoria Vinci. *Design and Human Factors Work of the Habitability Design Center for the International Space Station*. Prepared by the Habitability Design Center for NASA. Nassau Bay, Tex., n.d.

Fitchett, Joseph, Anthony Laurence, and Martin Meade. *Grand Oriental Hotels*. New York: Vendome, 1987.

Fruchtman, Brooke. "Canvas Creations." *I.D.* (November 2001): 21.

Gathje, Curtis. *At the Plaza: An Illustrated History of the World's Most Famous Hotel*. New York: St. Martin's Press, 2000.

Gueft, Olga. "Hotels in Warm Climes: Nassau Beach Lodge." *Interiors* (May 1959): 87–92.

Gordon, Meryl. "The Cool War." *New York Times*, May 27, 2001, Sunday magazine, 34–40.

Higley, Jeff, "'Boutique' Is Chic for Customer Service," *Hotel and Motel Management* (Mar. 5, 2001): 58–59.

"History of the Lodging Industry." *http://www.ahma.com/infocenter/lodging_history.asp*

Ho, Cathy Lang. "Curriculum Vito." *Architecture* (Jan. 2001): 51–54.

Ingram, Paul. *The Rise of Hotel Chains in the United States, 1896–1980*. New York and London: Garland Publishing, 1996.

Jarman, Rufus. *A Bed for the Night: The Story of the Wheeling Bellboy, E.M. Statler and His Remarkable Hotels*. New York: Harper and Brothers, 1952.

Kelts, Roland. "Soaplands and Love Hotels." *Salon (www.salon.com)* (Jan. 8, 2000).

Onion, Margaret Kent. "Drummers Accomodated: A Nineteenth Century Salesman in Minnesota." *Minnesota History* 46, 2 (1978): 59–65.

Kettmann, Steve. "Oil Realm Embraces a Wired Economy." *New York Times*, June 10, 2001, Business sec.

Kihn, Phyllis. "The American Hotel, 1845–1848." *Connecticut Historical Society Bulletin* 30, 1 (1965): 26–32.

Koch, Alexander. *Hotelbauten, Motels, Ferienhäuser*. Stuttgart, Germany: Koch, 1958.

Koolhaas, Rem. *Delirious New York: A Retroactive Manifesto for Manhattan*. New York: Oxford University Press, 1978. Reprint, Monacelli Press, 1995.

Koplos, Janet. "Toland Grinnell at Basilico." *Art in America* (Nov. 1998): 128.

Kurokawa, Kisho. "The Special Character of the Japanese Tradition." In Kurokawa, ed., *New Wave Japanese Architecture*. London: Academy Editions, 1993: 6–18.

———. *Kisho Kurokawa: Selected and Current Works. The Master Architect Series*. Victoria, B.C.: Images Publishing Group, 1995.

Lapidus, Morris. *Too Much Is Never Enough*. New York: Rizzoli International Publications, 1996.

Lefcowitz, Eric. *Golden Opportunities: 50 Years of Loews Hotels*. Bethesda: Custom News Celebration Publishing, 1996.

Lewis, Julia. "Peep Show." *Interior Design* (Oct. 2000): 140–43.

Limerick, Jeffery. *America's Grand Resort Hotels*. New York: Pantheon Books, 1979.

Lord, M. G. "Mars Needs Architects." *Dwell* (Aug. 2001): 66–71.

Louie, Elaine. "A Canvas the Artist Curls Up In." *New York Times*, July 5, 2001, House and Home sec.

Löfgren, Orvar. *On Holiday: A History of Vacationing*. Berkeley: University of California Press, 1999.

Matthew, Christopher. *A Different World: Great Stories of Hotels*. New York and London: Paddington Press, 1976.

McBride, Edward. "Burj al-Arab." *Architecture* (Aug. 2000): 116–25.

McKinley, Jesse. "It's Hopping in the Lobby as Hotels Party All Night." *New York Times*, Nov. 19, 2000, Styles sec.

Mencken, August. *The Railroad Passenger Car: An Illustrated History of the First One Hundred Years with Accounts by Contemporary Passengers*. Baltimore: Johns Hopkins Press, 1957.

Muschamp, Herbert. "Hotel Broadway: Architectural Trendsetter Seduces Historic Soho." *New York Times*, Apr. 11, 2001, Arts sec.

———. "Fitting into History's True Fabric." *New York Times*, May 6, 2001, Arts and Leisure sec.

Nobel, Philip. "Sheik Simple: The Burj al-Arab in Dubai is the World's Tallest, Most Opulent Hotel." *Interiors* (June 2000): 58–63.

Ogundehin, Michelle. "Schrager's Edge." *Interiors* (Sept. 2000): 84–89.

Pevsner, Nikolaus. *A History of Building Types*. Princeton, N.J.: Princeton University Press, 1976.

Raitz, Karl B., and John Paul Jones III. "The City Hotel as Landscape Artifact and Community Symbol." *Journal of Cultural Geography* 9, 1 (1988): 17–36.

Renzi, Jen. "Habitat for Humanity." *Interior Design* (Nov. 2000): 82–84

Ritchie, Matthew. "The Architecture of Possibility." *Performing Arts Journal* (Sept. 1996): 53–57.

Roberts, Michele. "Double Vision." *Tate: The Art Magazine* (Summer 2000): 43.

Roehl, Wesley S., and Carlton S. Van Doren. "Locational Characteristics of American Resort Hotels." *Journal of Cultural Geography* 11, 1 (1990): 71–83.

Ross, Michael Franklin. *Beyond Metabolism: The New Japanese Architecture*. New York: Architectural Record Books, 1978.

Russ, Sabine. "Extravagant Pragmatism: MK Kahne's Usable Art." In *MK Kahne: From Berlin No. 2* (New York: Janos Gat Gallery, 2001).

Sandoval-Strausz, A. K. "Why the Hotel? Liberal Visions, Merchant Capital, Public Space, and the Creation of an American Institution." *Business and Economic History*, 2d ser., 28, 2 (Winter 1999): 255–66.

Sowa, Axel. "Japanese Capsule Hotels." *L'Architecture d'Aujourd'hui* (June 2000): 84–87.

Sleeper, Harold. "Hotel Rooms: Design Standards and Data." *Architectural Forum* (Aug. 1954): 150–51.

Stephens, Suzanne. "The Hotel: Lucerne, Switzerland." *Architectural Record* (May 2001): 238–43.

———. "Project Diary: The Landmark PSFS Building by Bower Lewis Thrower Architects & Daroff Design Is Reincarnated as a Loews Hotel." *Architectural Record* (Oct. 2000): 136.

Stille, Alexander. "Globalization Now, A Sequel of Sorts." *New York Times*, Aug. 11, 2001, Business sec.

Stover, F. John. *The Routledge Historical Atlas of the American Railroad*. New York: Routledge, 1999.

Toland Grinnell: Trunks and Valises. New York: Sperone Westwater Gallery, 2001.

Tsao, Calvin. "Box Special." *V Magazine* 7 (Fall 2000): n.p.

Tyrnauer, Matt. "Hotel California." *Vanity Fair* (June 1999): 102–104ff.

Vanderbilt, Tom. "The Boutique Mystique." *Interiors* (June 2000): 68–77.

———. "This End Up." *Interiors* (Feb. 2001): 36–39.

Wharton, Annabel Jane. *Building the Cold War: Hilton International Hotels and Modern Architecture*. Chicago: University of Chicago Press, 2001.

Williams, Florence. "Putting a Room of One's Own in Orbit." *New York Times*, Dec. 30, 1999, Design 2002 sec.

Williamson, Jefferson. *The American Hotel: An Anecdotal History*. 1930. Reprint, New York: Arno Press, 1975.

BIOGRAPHIES OF ARCHITECTS AND DESIGNERS

Compiled by Randi Mates and Phyllis Ross

VITO ACCONCI

Born in the Bronx, New York, artist Vito Acconci has worked in and combined writing, performance art, film, and video. Since the late 1980s, with the founding of Acconci Studio, in Brooklyn, New York, he has focused his work on the design of public spaces, furniture, and vehicles, both built and theoretical. Recently built projects include a screened walkway for the Shibuya Station, Tokyo; a movable landscape for the courtyard of a government building in Munich; a Möbius strip bench in Fukuroi City, Japan; and a lighting system for the San Francisco Airport.

ARCHITECTURE RESEARCH OFFICE

Architecture Research Office (ARO) is an architecture practice in which individual projects are a vehicle for research into program, form, material, and construction. ARO's current projects include designing the installation of *New Hotels for Global Nomads* at Cooper-Hewitt, National Design Museum in New York, a War Remembrance Memorial at Columbia University, and private residences in New York City. The firm recently completed the Prada Store in Soho with Rem Koolhaas, the U.S. Armed Forces Recruiting Station in Times Square, and a flagship store for Shiseido, all in New York City. ARO's work has been widely published and has received awards from the American Institute of Architects, the Architectural League of New York, the New York City Arts Commission and the *I.D.* Annual Design Review.

W. S. ATKINS

W. S. Atkins is a London-based multinational, multivalent engineering firm with more than 140 offices worldwide. They provide their international clientele with guidance in engineering, architecture, transport, management, and property management when updating and implementing the technological and physical infrastructures of various municipalities, governments, and individual corporations.

ANDRÉ BALAZS

André Balazs is the owner of the Mercer Hotel in New York, the Chateau Marmont in Hollywood, and the Sunset Beach Hotel on Shelter Island, New York. Mr. Balazs has also created, owned, and operated numerous restaurants and nightclubs both in New York and Los Angeles. Prior to entering the entertainment and hospitality industry, Balazs was cofounder and executive vice president of Biomatrix, Inc., a biotechnology firm that pioneered the development of new biomaterials for injection in the human body.

RICHARD BARNES

San Francisco–based photographer Richard Barnes has work in the permanent collections of the San Francisco Museum of Modern Art, the Metropolitan Museum of Art, the Philadelphia Museum of Art, the Los Angeles County Museum of Art as well as in the Harvard Photographic Archive and the collections of Bank of America and Levi Strauss. His photographs for the *New York Times* of the cabin of the Unabomber, Theodore Kaczynski, earned him the prestigious Alfred Eisenstaedt Award in Photography in 1999.

DIKE BLAIR

Artist Dike Blair was born in New Castle, Pennsylvania, and lives in New York City. Since 1980 he has been the subject of more than twenty one-person exhibitions in the United States and Europe as well as group exhibitions at such museums as the Centre Georges Pompidou, the Walker Art Center, and the Whitney Museum of American Art. Blair has also written extensively about art and culture and is Associate Editor of *Purple* magazine.

BOWER LEWIS THROWER ARCHITECTS

Bower Lewis Thrower Architects is a Philadelphia firm serving the middle Atlantic region. During its forty-year history its practice has focused on urban projects for clients in the public and private sectors. It has been an innovator in the adaptation of historic structures for new uses. Its landmark 1970 master plan for Market Street East established the strategy for the renewal of a major portion of Philadelphia with a multilevel infrastructure linking retail, office, and transportation activities across six city blocks, the first such development in the country. The Pennsylvania Convention Center and the Loews Philadelphia Hotel are the most recent additions to this development.

SOPHIE CALLE

Parisian-born Sophie Calle is a conceptual artist and photographer. Her often autobiographical work began in the late 1970s. Calle's work explores seeing and being seen; she is famous for following strangers around cities and attempting to experience their lives vicariously by adopting their habits and their perceived personas. Recently, Calle has had solo exhibitions in Germany, Tokyo, New York, San Francisco, France, and England.

ANTONIO CITTERIO

Born in Medea, Italy, Milan-based designer Antonio Citterio received his architecture degree from the polytechnic university in Milan, Polytechnikum. Since 1972 he has worked as a product and industrial designer for such companies as Ansorg, Arclinea, B&B Italia, Pozzi e Ginori, Vitra, Kartell, and Flos. From 1987 to 1996, Citterio collaborated with Terry Dwan to develop both architectural projects and interiors including the headquarters and showrooms for Esprit in Milan, Amsterdam, and Antwerp. Citterio and Patricia Viel founded Antonio Citterio & Partners as a multidisciplinary practice for architecture, industrial design, and graphics in 1999. Citterio has work in the permanent collections of New York's Museum of Modern Art and the Centre Georges Pompidou, Paris.

MAUREEN CONNOR

Maureen Connor is an artist who lives in New York. She exhibits her work internationally and is represented by Leibman Magnan in New York and Galerie Sima in Nurenburg. Her most recent exhibitions include *Rapture* at the Barbican in London and *Individuals* at the Mendel Art Gallery in Saskatchewan, Canada, and the Tapies Foundation in Barcelona. She is a Professor of Art at Queens College in New York.

DAROFF DESIGN

Daroff Design, Inc., an interior design, architecture, and graphics firm specializing in hospitality and restaurant projects, was founded in 1973 by Karen Daroff. The firm's work has been published in *Interiors, Interior Design, Progressive Architecture, Architectural Record*, and other magazines. Daroff Design is currently ranked among the top ten hospitality design firms in the United States.

CARL DE SMET

Belgian Carl de Smet graduated with a laureate from the St. Lucas Institute in Brussels for a degree in experimental art. De Smet formed Uncontrollable Architectural Products in 1999 and, since then, has participated in a series of international architecture and design competitions.

DILLER + SCOFIDIO

Elizabeth Diller has been an Associate Professor of Architecture at Princeton since 1990. Her husband, Ricardo Scofidio, has been a professor of architecture at Cooper Union since 1965. In 1979 the pair founded Diller + Scofidio, also known as D + S. The firm's pursuits weave together architecture, electronic media (including video and digital installations), and advertising to explore the role of designed space in the modern, industrial world. In 1999 D + S received the MacArthur Foundation Award/Fellowship, the first time the prestigious award was given to architects. Recent works include the Blur Building in Switzerland (2002).

FAKESHOP

Taking their name from a phrase in an Alain Robbe-Grillet novel, the collective Fakeshop was founded in Brooklyn in 1997. Core member Jeff Gompertz, principal in the *Capsule Hotel*, seeks to materialize the sites of digital culture by creating environments, both physical and digital, which act as stagesets for the manifestations and repercussions of human and digital interactions. Fakeshop sees these arenas as the nexus of modern, urban experience.

fieldOFFICE

fieldOFFICE was founded by Annette Dudek and Jamie Meunier as a work group for design research. Based in New York City since 1998, they work across disciplines and through various media to expand the perimeters of traditional architectural practice. Their work has been exhibited at the 5th International Architecture Exhibition of the Venice Biennale, the Canadian Center for Architecture, and the Urban Isuue Gallery in Berlin. Both Dudek and Meunier hold B.Arch degrees from McGill University (1993), and Dudek has received an M.S. in Architectural History and Theory from the University of Pennsylvania (1997). Dudek is a faculty member in architectural design at the University of Pennsylvania, Pratt Institute, and Columbia and Barnard Colleges.

GARRETT FINNEY

Garrett Finney is Senior Architect at the Habitability Design Center, Johnson Space Center, Houston, where, since 1999, he has been working on designs for the Habitation Module of the International Space Station. His practice previously included designing houses and interiors and developing furniture prototypes for production. He has worked for a variety of firms including Kohn, Pedersen, Fox Associates, Turner Brooks, and Maya Lin. In 1994 he was awarded the Rome Prize in Architecture from the American Academy in Rome. In collaboration with his sister, Martha Finney, he has designed and built houses, which have been featured in magazines and books.

FTL

Todd Dalland and Nicholas Goldsmith are principals of FTL, a New York City design and engineering firm specializing in lightweight and deployable buildings. Founded in 1977 the firm has received numerous design awards and is known for its contributions to projects such as the Carlos Moseley Pavilion, which is used by the Metropolitan Opera to perform in parks in the New York metropolitan area, and the AT&T Global Olympic Village at the 1996 Olympics.

Current projects include a complex of traveling event buildings for Harley Davidson, and a retractable, inflated entrance airlock for the new NASA Space Shuttle.

TOLAND GRINNELL

New York–based artisan Toland Grinnell received his BA in Fine Arts at the School of Visual Arts, New York, in 1994. He is best known for his handmade luxury traveling cases containing elaborate fantasy-filled environs that attempt to address contemporary desires and seduction. His oeuvre includes works as diverse as the Gateway to Eternity installation in New York's Gramercy Park Hotel for Basilico Fine Arts at the Gramercy International Art Fair (1996) to a neo-renaissance globe swathed with nymphs, lions, and scrolls that decorates the entryway of the Venetian Hotel, Resort and Casino in Las Vegas.

SHAWN HAUSMAN

Shawn Hausman, born in California, began working on feature films at the age of seventeen and has completed work on fourteen films to date. Owner of New York City's famed 1980s nightclub Area, Hausman began his interior design career by working on commercial projects such as hotels and restaurants. Approaching interior design as very similar to designing a film set, Hausman focuses on creating spaces that reflect an imaginary narrative or "history" and employ dramatic uses of space to reflect the experiences possible within.

SPIKE JONZE

Spike Jonze was born Adam Spiegel in Potomac, Maryland. He began working in the skateboarding industry as a filmmaker and cofounded the Girl Skateboards company. Jonze began his print career in 1987 as an editor, writer, and photographer of *Freestylin', Go, BMX Action*, and *Homeboy*, a series of skateboarding and freestyle biking magazines. Presently, Jonze's writings and photography are featured in magazines like the Beastie Boys' *Grand Royal* and *Juxtapoz*. He garnered fame as the director of music videos by such varied groups as Sonic Youth, the Beastie Boys, Puff Daddy, Bjork, and REM. In 1999 Jonze directed the critically acclaimed film *Being John Malkovich*.

VLADIMIR KAGAN

Born in Rhine, Germany, Vladimir Kagan, now based in New York, has been a designer for more than half a century. His early work includes projects done for General Electric and Walt Disney as well the Delegates Cocktail Lounge at the first United Nations Headquarters in Lake Success, New York, in 1949. His work is in the permanent collections of the Brooklyn Museum of Art; The Victoria & Albert; the Vitra Design Museum; Cooper-Hewitt, National Design Museum; and the Die Neue Samlung. In 1999 Tom Ford, director of Gucci, chose to use Kagan's 1971 design for Omnibus Multi-level Seating System to furnish 364 Gucci stores.

M. K. KÄHNE

Born in Lithuania, Berlin-based artist M.K. Kähne began his career as a painter before developing his conceptual ideas into three-dimensional objects. His series *Sanitary Furniture* (Sanitärmobiliar) and *The Modern Man* (Der Moderne Mann) have been exhibited in Tokyo, New York, Madrid, and Berlin. Kähne has also participated in a number of group and solo exhibitions throughout Germany, Spain, and the United States.

KONING EIZENBERG

Julie Eizenberg and Hank Koning formed Koning Eizenberg Architecture, Inc., in 1982. The California architecture and planning firm is known for its imaginative, site-specific, and people-oriented design approach to buildings designed for everyday living, including affordable housing, community centers, schools, custom homes, hotels, stores, and workplaces. Koning Eizenberg have received numerous awards for their work including the Progressive Architecture First Award in 1987 for affordable housing in Santa Monica, and National AIA Honor Awards for the Simone Hotel (1994) and the 31st Street House (1996). The have also recently won two national competitions, one for a Children's Museum and another for a school in Chicago.

LEWIS.TSURUMAKI.LEWIS

Paul Lewis, Marc Tsurumaki, and David J. Lewis began their architectural collaboration in 1992 in New York City. Their studio is committed to exploring the creative possibilities of architecture through a close examination of the conventional and ordinary, recasting the restrictions of each project as catalysts for invention. The firm has designed and fabricated office and exhibition spaces for the Van Alen Institute, Princeton Architectural Press, and Happy Mazza Media Company. In 2000 they were selected by *Architectural Record* as one of ten young firms that comprise a "new vanguard" in architecture and participated in Cooper-Hewitt, National Design Museum's *National Design Triennial*. Works in progress include the Lozoo Restaurant, New York City, and Bornhuetter Hall, a residence hall for the College of Wooster, Wooster, Ohio. They are the authors of *Pamphlet Architecture 21: Snafu* (1999), and have received three *I.D. Magazine* design awards. All three are professors of architecture.

PETER MARLOW

British photojournalist Peter Marlow began his career in the 1970s at the Sygma Agency where he covered world news events in such places as Lebanon and Northern Ireland. By 1980 Marlow moved beyond photojournalism to explore the visual aspects of the medium, using his subjects to examine social issues. Marlow became a member of Magnum in 1980 and served as president of the cooperative from 1990 to 1994. Marlow is renowned for his Amiens series, which examines the character of a small French town, done in the 1980s, and Non Places, which looks at the so-called detritus of English landscape and culture, shot in the 1990s. Recent solo exhibitions include *Non Places* (1998), *Nantes* (2001), and *In the Steps of George Rodger* (2002). Marlow's photographs are in the collections of the Arts Council of Great Britain, The Victoria and Albert Museum, and the Centre National de la Photographie, Paris.

nARCHITECTS

nARCHITECTS is a New York firm formed in 1999 by Eric Bunge and Mimi Hoang. They recently won the Architectural League's Young Architects Forum Prize in 2001, and their work has been exhibited at New York City's Urban Center, the Municipal Gallery in Ottawa, and ArchiLab 2002 in Orléans, France. Bunge is a faculty member at Parsons School of Design, Columbia University, and Barnard College. Hoang has worked at Steven Holl Architects on the Nelson Atkins Museum in Kansas City and a dormitory for MIT. Both Bunge and Hoang graduated from the Harvard Graduate School of Design.

JEAN NOUVEL

Born in Fumel, France, architect Jean Nouvel began designing in 1970 and graduated from the Ecole des Beaux Arts in 1972. He has won, among others, the Gold Medal of the French Academy of Architecture, the Royal Gold Medal of the Royal Institute of British Architects, the Aga Khan Prize, honorary fellowships in the Royal Institute of British Architects and the American Institute of Architects, France's National Grand Prize for Architecture, and, in 2001, Italy's Borromini Prize and Japan's Praemium Imperial Career Prize. His most renowned commissions include the Foundation Cartier building (Paris, 1994), the Arab World Institute/ Institut du Monde Arabe (Paris, 1987), and the Galeries Lafayette department store in Berlin.

ROCKWELL GROUP

In 1983 David Rockwell created Rockwell Group, a broad-based architectural practice with theatrically inspired projects. The ninety-person firm specializes in "entertainment architecture" for clients such as the Walt Disney Company, Sony/Loews Theaters, Planet Hollywood and other theme restaurants, the Mohegan Sun Casino, and Cirque du Soleil. Recent and current projects include a new facility for the Theater for the Academy of Motion Picture Arts and Sciences, Los Angeles, and the Mohegan Sun Casino Phase II in Connecticut. The W New York received *Interiors* magazine's design award for best hotel project in 2000.

HANS-JURGEN ROMBAUT

Dutch architect Hans-Jurgen Rombaut, based in the Netherlands, trained in both engineering and architecture. He has worked as a freelance architect since completing studies at the Academy of Architecture and Urban Design in Rotterdam. Focusing mainly on urban dwelling projects, he has specialized in ecological building design. He has also been involved in theoretical projects for building in extreme environments, especially in space.

ROY

Born in South Africa, architect Lindy Roy founded ROY in New York City in 2000. The studio's projects for eco-resort, residential, commercial, and entertainment environments have received wide attention in the design press. Ms. Roy has combined teaching with professional practice, lecturing most recently at Princeton University, Cooper Union, and Columbia University. Until 1995 she worked in the studios of Peter Eisenman Architects. In 2001 Ms. Roy was the winner of the Museum of Modern Art's Young Architects Competition. She is the youngest of thirty-three architects selected by Richard Meier to participate in the prestigious Houses at Saga-ponac development project.

TOM SACHS

Artist-bricoleur Tom Sachs is based in New York City. Since 1993 his work has appeared in a dozen solo exhibitions and more than thirty group exhibitions in American, European, and Japanese galleries and museums. His work is included in the permanent collections of the Whitney Museum of American Art, the Solomon R. Guggenheim Museum, the Museum of Modern Art (New York), the San Francisco Museum of Modern Art, and the Metropolitan Museum of Art Costume Institute, as well as in numerous private collections. His sculptures, which he describes as "cultural prosthetics," are inspired and influenced by commercialism and technology. His work *Sony Outsider* was the subject of an exhibition and catalog produced by SITE Santa Fe in 1999.

JOEL SANDERS

Joel Sanders received his M.Arch. from Columbia University and was a designer at Kohn Pedersen Fox before opening Joel Sanders Architect in 1987. Sanders, an associate professor at Yale University, was the director of the graduate program at Parsons School of Design, New York, from 1996 to 2001. Editor of *Stud: Architectures of Masculinity* (1996), Sanders frequently writes about art and design, most recently in *Art Forum* and the *Harvard Design Review*. His work is in the permanent collec-

tions of the Museum of Modern Art (New York), the San Francisco Museum of Modern Art, and the Carnegie Museum of Art (Pittsburgh). Recent projects include House for a Bachelor, which was part of the *Unprivate House* exhibition at MoMA in 1999, and the Access House, St. Simons Island, Georgia, which was included in the exhibition *Big Brother: Architecture and Surveillance* at the Museum of Contemporary Art in Athens, Greece.

IAN SCHRAGER

Ian Schrager is chairman and CEO of Ian Schrager Hotels, which owns and operates nine properties in New York, Miami, Los Angeles, San Francisco, and London. Hotels currently under development include the Empire, Astor Place, and Bond Street in New York; the Miramar, a resort village and wellness spa, in Santa Barbara, California; a second hotel in Miami Beach; and a hotel-apartment-entertainment complex in South America. With his late partner Steve Rubell, Schrager created Studio 54 and Palladium, legendary New York nightspots of the 1970s and 1980s, and together they developed their first hotel project in 1984. Since then, the sophistication, high-style design, and clublike bars and restaurants of these "urban resorts" have come to define the quintessential boutique hotel.

SERVO

Founded in 1999, Servo is a research and design collaborative established by David Erdman (Los Angeles), Marcelyn Gow (Zurich), Ulrika Karlsson (Stockholm), and Chris Perry (New York), whose work focuses on the integration of new media and mass production in the practice of architecture. Servo's work has been featured in four solo exhibitions in the United States and Europe and in several group exhibitions. In addition, the partners regularly teach and lecture in Europe and the U.S. Their work was included in *Young Architects Forum*, the Architectural League of New York (2001), and in *Mood River*, a group exhibition at Wexner Center for Contemporary Art, Columbus, Ohio (2002).

PHILIPPE STARCK

French-born Philippe Starck has earned critical acclaim for more than twenty-five years for his designs of architecture, interiors, and products. His varied achievements include redecorating the Elysées Palace at the request of French President Francois Mitterrand and being the consulting designer for Ian Schrager Hotels. Recent projects include The Hudson (2000) and Clift (2001) hotels and the Restaurant Bon in Paris (2000).

BARRY STERNLICHT

Barry Sternlicht is chairman and CEO of Starwood Hotels & Resorts Worldwide Inc., one of the largest hotel companies in the world. Starwood owns more than 750 properties in eighty countries and such brands as Sheraton, Westin, St. Regis, and W.

JONATHAN M. TISCH

Since 1989 Jonathan M. Tisch has been chairman and CEO of Loews Hotels. In addition to focusing on the company's growth as a leading luxury hotel chain, he is actively involved in many cultural, social, and business organizations. He is chairman of the Travel Business Roundtable, a coalition of executives representing the travel and tourism industry. Tisch serves on the Board of NYC & Company, the local convention and visitors bureau. His numerous honors and awards include "Hotel Person of the Year," from *Travel Agent* magazine, and being named to the Top 25 Travel Executives of 2001 by *Business Travel News*.

DRE WAPENAAR

Netherlander Dre Wapenaar received his Master's degree from the Academy of Visual Arts in Tilburg in 1986. Trained as a sculptor, Wapenaar began designing tents as a way to create work that was functional and resonant for all audiences. Wapanaar has exhibited work in the Netherlands, England, Italy, the U.S., France, and Japan. Recent work includes *Hang, Kiss, Smoke* (The Netherlands, 2001) and *DeathBivouac* (Amsterdam, 2002).

Donald Albrecht is an independent curator, architect, and writer who is Exhibitions Curator at Cooper-Hewitt, National Design Museum in New York. He was exhibition director and catalog editor of *The Work of Charles and Ray Eames: A Legacy of Invention*.

FRONT COVER: The Hotel, Lucerne, Switzerland, 2000, Ateliers Jean Nouvel. *Photo*: Philippe Ruault. BACK COVER: Capsule Hotel, 2002, Jeff Gompertz, fakeshop. *Photos and video tech*: Julieta Aranda.

OTHER TITLES FROM MERRELL PUBLISHERS

Modern Trains and Splendid Stations:
Architecture, Design, and Rail Travel for the Twenty-First Century
ISBN 1 85894 149 0

New London Architecture
ISBN 1 85894 150 4

Contemporary Rugs: Art and Design
ISBN 1 85894 164 4

Merrell Publishers Limited
42 Southwark Street
London SE1 1UN
www.merrellpublishers.com

Printed and bound in Italy
ISBN 1 85894 174 1

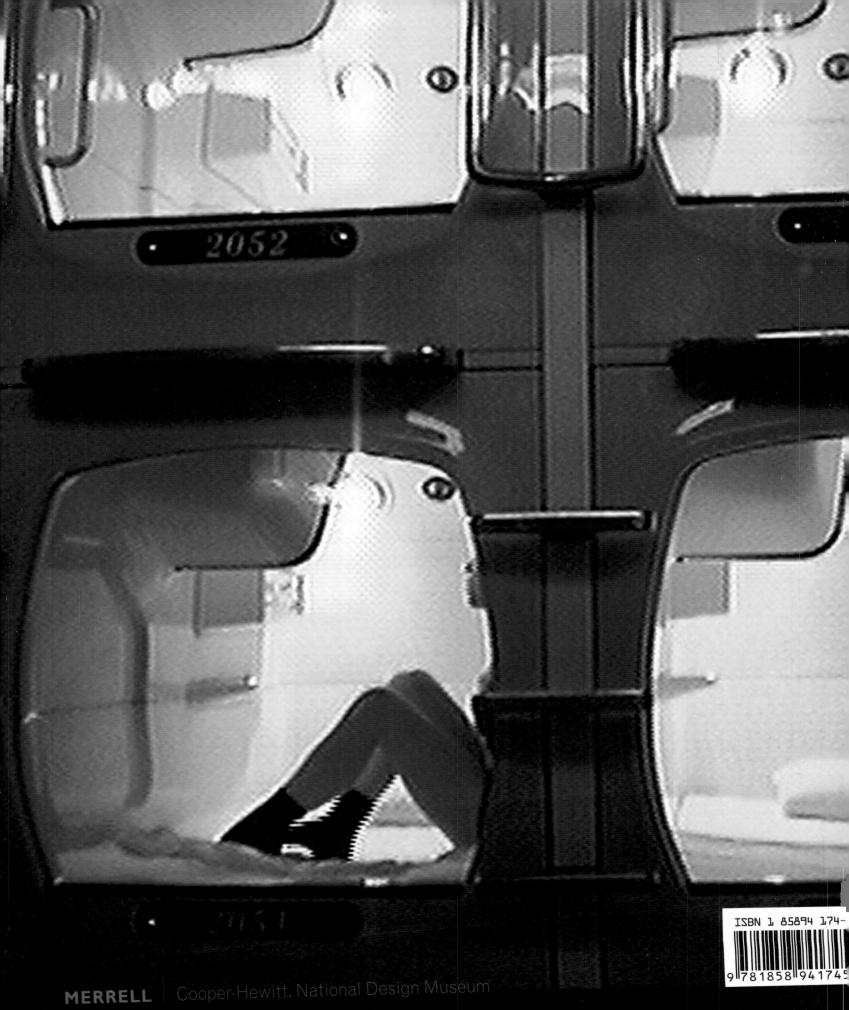

2052

MERRELL | Cooper-Hewitt, National Design Museum

ISBN 1 85894 174-

9 781858 941745